SUCCESSFUL
SERVANT
LEADERSHIP

Insights from Servant Leaders in
EDUCATION, BUSINESS,
HEALTHCARE, POLITICS,
ATHLETICS & RELIGION

Gerald Baldner

D.B. Reinhart Institute for Ethics in Leadership

VITERBO UNIVERSITY
LA CROSSE, WISCONSIN

ISBN 13: 978-0-9816896-6-1

D.B. Reinhart Institute for Ethics in Leadership
Viterbo University
900 Viterbo Drive
La Crosse, WI 54601
www.viterbo.edu/ethics

The D.B. Reinhart Institute for Ethics in Leadership is located on the campus of Viterbo University in La Crosse, Wisconsin. Its mission is to promote the concept of ethics in leadership as integral to the advancement of American society and to advance leadership and ethics through publications, courses, conferences, workshops, and public forums.

I dedicate this book to our son
JASON TODD BALDNER
whom we greatly miss.

April 18, 1975– July 28, 2010

Contents

Forward by Thomas Thibodeau ix

Acknowledgments xi

A Journey Begins 3

Our Roadmap for Servant Leadership 9

A Difficult Start Along the Road 15

Warm Fuzzies and Cold Pricklies 21

Paying It Forward 27

Signposts of Success 31

Servant Leadership in Education 35

JERRY KEMBER 37

RICK ARTMAN 50

DARRYLE CLOTT 63

Servant Leadership in Business 75

DON WEBER 77

JANET STANSFIELD HESS 88

KRISTINA (SMABY) SCHOH 103

Servant Leadership in Healthcare 115

DR. JEFF THOMPSON 117

AMANDA BUCKLES 136

Servant Leadership in Politics 151

GOV. TOMMY THOMPSON 153

SPEAKER DENNIS HASTERT 167

Servant Leadership in Athletics   183
    ROGER HARRING   184
    BARBARA GIBSON   192
Servant Leadership in Religion   209
    PASTOR BILL HYBELS   211
A Little Side Trip: ST. FRANCIS OF ASSISI   221
The Journey Is Coming to an End   233

Afterword   239

Foreword

by Thomas Thibodeau

To be a good storyteller, one first has to be a good story-listener. The stories of servant leaders that you will read and reflect on in this book are told by a remarkable story-listener, Gerald Baldner. Gerald has a contemplative spirit and understanding of service and leadership. His grounding came from his family farm in rural Minnesota. He further developed his skills of listening and understanding as a social work supervisor and as the Director of Special Education in an Iowa school district.

His listening abilities grew as he taught in a Viterbo University classroom. He listened to his own heart, his wife, and God as his vocation led him to begin ten successful businesses. In each business he listened to his guests', co-workers', and employees' needs and then worked with humility, joy, and discipline to meet those needs. As Robert Greenleaf, the modern-day father of servant leadership, writes, "The servant leader is servant first . . . It begins with the natural feeling that one wants to serve, to serve first." Gerald has always served; it is his nature to be a servant. "Then conscious choice brings one to aspire to lead," Greenleaf observes. Gerald has become such a leader. It was only natural for him to be drawn to servant leadership as his way of life. He also found that the wanted to tell the stories of others who were called to serve and lead.

He telephoned, wrote letters, and sent e-mails to invite people to tell their stories about service and leadership. He listened and crafted the narratives that capture the spirit of servant leadership as it is lived out daily by ordinary servant leaders. In these stories, we find our life stories amplified and celebrated. We are reminded of our common work to serve and lead others for the common good.

Gerald is a friend of mine. He has inspired me to be a better husband, father, teacher, and servant leader. I trust he will do the same for you in the stories he has listened to and told.

> *Do what is necessary;*
> *Then do what is possible,*
> *And then soon you will find yourself*
> *Doing the impossible.*
> —St. Francis of Assisi

THOMAS THIBODEAU
Director of the Masters Program in Servant Leadership
Distinguished Professor of Servant Leadership
Viterbo University

Acknowledgments

Writing a book takes a lot of time and patience, and it is impossible to do without the help and support of many people.

I would first of all like to thank the very wonderful and gracious individuals who allowed me to interview them: Jerry Kember, Darryle Clott, Rick Artman, Don Weber, Janet Stansfield Hess, Kristina (Smaby) Schoh, Jeff Thompson, Amanda Buckles, Tommy Thompson, Dennis Hastert, Roger Harring, Barbara Gibson, and Bill Hybel.

A big thank you to my wife, Betty, for putting up with my impatience and, at times, stress and for her initial typing and editing of my words.

I am very appreciative of the counsel, wisdom, and advice from Tom Thibodeau and very grateful for the numerous times spent with Rick Kyte and for his guidance and suggestions all along the way toward completing this project.

My last acknowledgement and appreciation goes to my good friend Judy Kirkpatrick. Thank you so much for all of your suggestions and positive comments along the way. Thank you for smoothing out the rough edges and for all of your transcribing.

I could not have completed this project without you. The completion of this project was a collaborative effort, and I am very grateful to everyone who helped to make it a reality.

Successful Servant Leadership

A Journey Begins

When I was about seven years old, I was in the front seat of our pick-up truck, and I remember watching as my father finished up a formal agreement with a neighboring farmer by shaking hands. After that incident, I observed on many occasions his sealing a deal with someone by shaking their hands. Although I probably couldn't have put it into words at the time, somehow I knew that my father and whomever he was conducting business with had a strong relationship based on mutual trust. There was an aura of respect and honesty that implied they were both good for their word.

In both his business and personal life, my father was a living example of goodness, kindness, and honesty, and the way he conducted himself had a huge impact on me. As a farmer, he planted crops. As a father, he established in me the roots of trusting and respecting others, and they are strong roots in me even today. Until someone has proven otherwise, I tend to trust everyone with whom I come in contact, and this has served me well in my career. Naturally, there have been a few exceptions—times when I "got burned" and trust was misplaced—but the recovery from those instances was usually quick, and I almost always managed to turn them into learning experiences

As I look back on my growing-up years, I never thought of my father as a mentor or role model. He was just my father. Our family never thought of him as a "Servant Leader." He was just our father, my mom's husband, a friend to many. But as I have come to study the concept of Servant Leadership and its characteristics, I now recognize that my father was a true Servant Leader and that he instilled in me the roots to develop into a Servant Leader.

There have been Servant Leaders for thousands of years, but not until recently have they been referred to as such. We now have a term that describes someone who exhibits—and puts into practice—the virtuous qualities of life. The framework of a Servant Leader has been fleshed out until we now have a defined concept to aspire to. It is with that intent that I decided to write this book. It is my hope and prayer that by examining the lives and careers of other Servant Leaders we can learn and improve the content and quality of our own lives and those of others.

Because my father and the life he led had such a profound impact on the way I chose to live my life, I offer the following words that I read at my father's funeral (he was ninety-eight years old):

> We always knew that Dad was a special person. It was obvious to us and to anyone that came in contact with him that he was a genuine, caring, loving, and sensitive human being. He never strived to be something other than who he was. He showed us how to live life to its fullest and demonstrated a love of life that was contagious. As children growing up in a farming community, we can remember the gentle touch of his strong and firm hand. He exemplified the value of working hard and at the same time showed how to look forward to reaping the fruits of his labor.
>
> While he was a loving father to us, we appreciated the kind of husband he was to our mother and the wonderful role model that he represented to our children.
>
> However, it was not until after he lost his eyesight twenty-five years ago that his greatest characteristics came to the surface. It was his ability to accept whatever adversity comes to life that inspired us the most. He accepted his unwanted disability with the virtuous character of a saint. It

was his ability to discourage pity that made you feel like you were in the presence of a special human being.

We will miss you, Dad, but we know that right now you are where you want to be. Now we know that once again you can see us all and that you now can see the grandchildren that you only knew by sound or touch. Your smile, your engaging life, your gentleness and love will remain forever in our hearts and minds.

I suspect some of you may be wondering why I would begin a book on Servant Leadership by referencing a story about my father. While I'm sure he never heard or read the words "servant" and "leadership" used together, I am convinced he practiced Servant Leadership. We never talked about what we have now come to know as Servant Leadership. We never encouraged each other to put into practice the defined characteristics of Servant Leadership.

The initial impetus for me to write this book is that I believe that if we better understand Servant Leadership and encourage each other to practice Servant Leadership principles, we will indeed become better Servant Leaders. In an attempt to better explain what I am trying to say, I am going to share an analogy that, I hope, will help draw a connection.

For many years, approximately thirty-five, I have been playing what we call noon-hour basketball with good friends and, in most cases, athletes, who either played junior high, high school, or even in some cases college basketball. Some of the original noon-hour basketball players, very good friends of mine, are still able to get up and down the floor (however, certainly not as fast as we used to). I have made many good friends from this wonderful source of camaraderie and in the process helped to stay in good physical condition.

After we decide which teams each person is going to be on, usually identified by dark shirts or white shirts, we begin to play. During the course of our game, there are some good passes delivered, some good shots made, and rebounds gathered in, as we jump two inches off the floor (maybe that is a stretch), etc. We have some very good games, and you can definitely tell that our competitive nature has not escaped us as much as our athletic abilities.

If you were to watch these games, you would soon observe that we do not have any pre-planned plays that guide us in what we do, and no one really knows where he should be on the court, yet we still have fun.

Here's my point. If one of the teams was given some structure to their play, if they were coached about where they should be on the court, if they knew where their teammates were going to be, if they set screens for each other (believe it or not, sometimes we do), and if they practiced those things, they would have a better memory and understanding of what they should do. They would become a much better team, and I suspect their opponents would be no competition at all.

I believe that if we better-defined and understood what the concept of Servant Leadership is, and if we practiced the principles and characteristics of Servant Leadership, we would all benefit from the results. It is my core belief that if we want to become better at what we do, we must first have a roadmap of how we plan to get there.

As you continue to read this book, and I certainly hope you do, you'll probably realize that I am not an especially proficient writer, nor do I aspire to be. I simply write from the heart and use the words that I speak in my everyday life. I use very few words that you will have to look up in the dictionary. The words I use are the ones I have always used in my quest to become a Servant Leader.

Our Road Map
for Servant Leadership

Come on a journey with me. *Destination:* Servant Leadership.

Today, as many of us travel, we have the benefit of a Global Positioning System (GPS). Enter a desired destination, and our GPS tells us what route to take, which highways and streets to follow when we are off course and in unverified territory, and even an estimate of how long it will take us to get to our final destination. In this case, I don't have the benefit of computer technology, but I do hope that this journey takes us from little or no understanding of what Servant Leadership means to a clear comprehension and application of the principles and characteristics of Servant Leadership. And because writing a book is as much a journey as reading one, this is a journey for me, as well. It is a journey for me to understand how meaningful Servant Leadership may be in our society.

Usually when we begin a journey, we have a good idea of where we are going and how we are going to get there. However, in this case I'm not sure what path I will follow or what detours may occur along the way. But I do know I have to start with the basics.

In many areas across the country the concept of Servant Leadership is not very well known or understood. In the community in which I live (La Crosse, Wisconsin), the concept of Servant Leadership is probably better known and understood than in most areas, because Viterbo University, a local university, has created a Master's Degree program in Servant Leadership.

So what is known about Servant Leadership? Essentially, Servant Leadership is an all-encompassing concept that includes many virtues and values. In a sense, it is an umbrella under which positive values, ethics, and virtues all come into play. It is not just about being honest, courteous, respectful, understanding, or trustworthy. Rather it is a combination of all these values, plus many more.

The "father" of Servant Leadership, Robert K. Greenleaf, defined Servant Leadership as follows:

> The Servant Leader is servant first. It begins with a natural feeling that one wants to serve, to serve first. Then conscious choice brings one to aspire to lead. That person is sharply different from one who is leader first, perhaps because of the need

to assume an unusual power drive or to acquire material possessions. The leader-first and the servant-first are two extreme types. Between them there are shadings and blends that are part of the independent variety of human nature.

The difference manifests itself in the care taken by the servant-first to make sure that other people's highest priority needs are being served. The best test, and difficult to administer, is: Do those served grow as persons? Do they, while being served, become healthier, wiser, freer, more autonomous, more likely themselves to become servants? And, what is the effect on the least privileged in society? Will they benefit or at least not be further deprived?

With my initial reading and research, I began to realize how valuable this way of life can be in our society and in our world. I decided to dig beneath the surface to find out where the roots of Servant Leadership come from, and whether or not the principles and characteristics of Servant Leadership can be learned or taught. Is it something inherent in an individual's ethical DNA, or can it be observed, practiced, and absorbed until it is second nature?

"You Have Strayed off Course"

Let's take a little detour here. As we travel on this journey, and as you learn more about Servant Leadership, I want you to keep these questions in mind:

1. Do you think you use Servant Leadership characteristics and principles in your roles in life?

2. Would you like to improve your implementation of Servant Leadership principles?

3. Can you think of other people you consider to be Servant Leaders?

One thought as I began my journey toward a better understanding of this all-encompassing concept was that Servant Leadership was not just a religious idea nor was it specifically assigned to any one vocation, discipline, or career. Indeed, Servant Leadership principles and characteristics can be applied to all walks of life.

We will examine how these principles have been applied to daily life and how they have helped many people become successful in the areas of business, athletics, education, healthcare, religion, and politics.

As I began writing this book, I was very excited

about putting my thoughts into print on this very meaningful concept, because I knew it was something about which I could become passionate. But as I began the research, I realized that there had been much more written about Servant Leadership than I had suspected, and panic set in. How and in what ways could I say something about Servant Leadership that had not already been said? Then I reminded myself about how many books have been written on Positive Mental Attitude, Business Management, Healthcare, etc., each one offering a different perspective or application. I realized that the number of books written about Servant Leadership was minor by comparison, and my enthusiasm returned, along with the desire to promote and inform people and to raise the level of awareness about Servant Leadership.

A Difficult Start
Along the Road

To help you understand what prompted my initial desire to explore and write about Servant Leadership, I must share a sequence of events that took place in my life during the summer and fall of 2010.

As you may have noticed, I have dedicated this journey to my son, Jason. Jason was involved in a serious boating accident on May 8, 2010 and remained in a coma for eighty-one days. Many times during those very difficult days we thought that he would emerge from his coma, but he never did. He was taken from us on July 28, 2010.

The time between his accident and his death were emotionally excruciating for my family and his many friends. I spent many nights in a lounge chair next to his bed, and I was with him the night before he died. I had just left the hospital on the morning of July 28, and before I returned home, my wife, Betty, was called with the news that he had taken his last breath.

As a result of trying to deal with our grief, Betty and I sought the help of a grief counselor. One of her suggestions was that we needed to become involved in something about which we could become passionate. She suggested that becoming involved in something that could consume our minds and actions could help us emerge from our paralyzing state of grief. I spent a lot of time thinking and praying about it, but I couldn't imagine anything that would distract me from the thought of never being able to see our son again.

In the weeks that followed Jason's passing, it became more difficult every day for me to go to work. I owned a company called Kitchen Solvers, a kitchen remodeling company that Betty and I started from the ground up in 1982 as a retail outlet. In 1984, I began to franchise Kitchen Solvers, and today we have just under one-hundred franchises in multiple states and Canada.

As much as Kitchen Solvers meant to me, I knew it was time to move on and to focus on other things. I was fortunate to have a number of potential buyers, and eventually I decided on two gentlemen from the La Crosse area. They each demonstrated the kind of business principles and characteristics that I was looking for. We reached an agreement and set the date of December 1, 2010 for completing the sale.

Prior to the closing, I wanted my staff and the new owners to get to know each other. We scheduled a meeting, and I asked the prospective owners to introduce themselves and to explain their interest in becoming a part of this twenty-eight-year-old business. They had put together an agenda and introduction of their own, and I was pleased and surprised to see that they wanted to discuss with the staff how to move forward with our existing franchises using the principles of Servant Leadership!

When I mentioned to the new owners how pleased I was that they had considered Servant Leadership to be an important concept to pursue, our general manager looked at me and said, "Gerald, you have used Servant Leadership principles your whole business life, and that's why you have been successful."

Naturally, his statement meant a lot to me, and that evening I thought about what he said. I had never really thought of myself as a Servant Leader, but I began to reflect on the fact that I had successfully started several businesses since 1982, and the common factors they shared were the manner in which I did business, the ethical code that guided my actions, and the way I dealt with people.

My companies included The Cabinet Factory (now called Walzcraft), a manufacturer of kitchen cabinet and bathroom components. I sold it to my very capable partner who continued to grow the business. There was Creative Laminates, a manufacturer of casework products, which I sold to my daughter and her husband, and which continues to grow and thrive. I still retain ownership in Counter Creations, a fabricator of solid surface products, and B&T Properties, a land development company. We sold Kitchen Solvers (retail division) to a young couple who had worked for us prior to making the purchase. They have also continued to grow and maintain a positive reputation in our community. And then, as I said previously, I sold the Kitchen Solvers franchise company to two very capable young men who I know will be successful in expanding that company.

The point of including this brief "resumé" is to illustrate that I had started and grown these businesses utilizing Servant Leadership principles, and all of them have continued to grow and prosper. It all ties together.

As I reflected on the risks and stress that were involved in starting, running, and growing these businesses, I realized that indeed I had used some Servant Leadership values and principles. As is true in any business, things do not always go as we plan; everyone does not always agree with the owner's ideas. Thinking about some of those diverse situations and times of conflict, I considered the values I had used in an attempt to resolve them.

For many years, I enjoyed the support and loyalty of my partners, associates, and employees, and yet I also know that there were times when Servant Leadership principles were absent in my dealings with people. Still, I would like to think that in those situations when I sensed that I did not have complete trust or loyalty, I did what was necessary to correct it. I am also sure there were still times when I was not totally successful in a achieving those goals.

As all of these thoughts were going through my mind that night, I could not sleep because I was excited about the possibility of writing a book on Servant Leadership. I knew that this was a subject about which I could become passionate, but there were many questions. Could I write such a book? How could I say what I wanted to say? What examples could I use? The questions went on and on, and for the first time in many months I could not sleep because I was excited about something, a stark contrast to all the sleepless nights I had experienced just prior to that.

Since starting this journey, I've had some curves and ruts in the road. I still face the daily grief and sense of loss of Jason. But it has become evident to me that this new passion and focus is a life-altering event. There are many people I know who have used Servant Leadership principles and characteristics in their given roles in life, and I want to talk with them, perhaps learn from them. Many of these people are personal heroes to me, and I know that I will benefit from getting to know them better and, at the same time, develop a much better understanding about the positive components of this way of life that I hope to pass on to others.

Warm Fuzzies
and Cold Pricklies

I am going to take a slight detour here and veer off the designated path on our journey. Uh-oh, I can just hear my GPS system saying, "You have now entered unverified territory; please check your surroundings." I am taking this detour in an attempt to create a better understanding and application of Servant Leadership principals.

When I was a school social worker in 1973, I was asked by the principal of a small elementary school in northeast Iowa to help a teacher whose class of fifth graders was, by her own description, the most difficult class she had ever taught. She said her students were totally insensitive to the feelings of their peers, cruel in their comments to each other, and that they had no concern about how they were negatively affecting the lives, and more importantly, the emotions and feelings, of their classmates.

With the teacher's cooperation I implemented a behavioral modification program in an attempt to change the attitudes and the stormy conflict in her classroom. As a backdrop to the program I wanted to implement a reference to a children's story called

"A Warm Fuzzy Tale," written by Claude M. Steiner in 1969. The story focuses on a small make-believe community where everyone was given a small soft fuzzy bag when they were born. Anytime a person reached into this bag, they were able to pull out a "warm fuzzy." Warm fuzzies were very much in demand, because whenever someone was given a warm fuzzy it made them feel warm and fuzzy all over and good about themselves. This make-believe fiction story continues by describing the use of "cold pricklies" as the antithesis of warm fuzzies. Cold pricklies were symbolic medals that made their recipients feel cold and prickly all over, which made them feel very sad.

Incorporating the overall message of this story as a basis for my comments on a Monday morning, I explained to the students the importance of being respectful and sensitive to the feelings of one another, and that how we treat each other affects our feelings of self-worth. I explained that for one week we were going to think about how and why we offended or hurt someone's feelings (cold pricklies), and how the opposite effect could take place when we are kind, respectful, or courteous to one another (warm fuzzies).

After discussing appropriate classroom behavior, I handed each student a red construction paper circle badge (which stood for cold pricklies), a green construction paper circle badge (which stood for warm fuzzies), and two safety pins. I explained to them that each day that week they would place these two circle badges on their shirt or blouse. Every time someone did something that hurt their feelings, that was rude, offensive, or hurtful, they would go to that person and put a check mark along with their name on the cold prickly badge. Alternatively, I asked that any time a person said something or did something to them that made them feel good about themselves, they should go to that person and place a check mark and their name on their warm fuzzy badge.

At the end of the day the teacher was to collect all the badges and tally the number of cold prickly and warm fuzzy checkmarks.

The teacher and I came up with several positive or negative consequences for the number of check marks each received on their cold prickly or warm fuzzy badge. Negative consequences included having no recess, cleaning the blackboard, and sitting apart from other students in the classroom. Conversely, if a student had one-to-three checks on their warm fuzzy badge, he or she might enjoy being awarded longer recess, playing games during class, receiving candy, and so forth.

Understandably, and by design, students initially thought of this program as sort of a game. It wasn't as important how they viewed the program as it was that it made them aware and conscious of their own behavior. At the end of the week, I had a dialogue with the students to discuss their feelings about what took place that week. The comments were very interesting and informative, and indeed, it appeared that it had raised their level of awareness about the effects of their good and bad behavior. The program was viewed as a tremendous success by the principal, teacher, and students, and later was highlighted in an Iowa education journal.

I feel there are a lot of similarities to practicing Servant Leadership principles and the use of warm fuzzies. Because many readers previously may not have a clear understanding of Servant Leadership, it is my hope that understanding and awareness of the principles of Servant Leadership (those warm fuzzies!) will lead to a more conscious effort and attempt to practice them.

Just a quick note: During the week that the behavioral modification program was in place, I kept my family informed about what was taking place in this fifth-grade classroom. We had fun with this concept at home, as well. Oftentimes, we would say to members of our family that they had just given us a warm fuzzy and thanked them for it. We also informed them when they had just given us a cold prickly. If you are a parent of children still living at home, I encourage you to experiment with this unique way of informing each other about their appropriate or inappropriate behavior. It is a positive and non-confrontational way of informing people about how their behavior affects others.

Paying It Forward

The promotion and application of Servant Leadership in our lives and in the lives of others has the potential to positively change the world.

Wow! Do you really think so? Do you really believe that? Who said that?

I did. Just like many others who are also saying it, I really believe it to be true. It is that conviction that continues to propel me on this journey.

In my eager attempt to present a better understanding of Servant Leadership, I am going to veer off my initial path once again and take you to the movies.

When I began to research the concept of Servant Leadership and the positive effects it can have on individuals, businesses, nonprofit organizations, and communities, I remembered a movie that I had seen several years ago called *Pay It Forward*. You too may have seen this movie or read the book.

Watching this film once more, I was quickly reminded why I had such positive memories about the plot and the feelings and emotions that the director and actors portray in this fictional story. The story begins with a very intellectual and confident teacher who is quite self-conscious because of some physical deformities that he suffered in a fire. He begins the first day of his class by telling students that, if they wanted some extra credit to improve their grades, they could participate in a special assignment. The assignment? What could they do to positively change the world? A few of his sixth-graders responded to this challenge, but one student in particular takes the assignment very seriously. His idea of how to positively change the world was based on a theory he called "pay it forward." The idea was to do a random good deed for three people, then ask each of them to also do a random good deed for three other people. In the book and movie this unbelievably simple theory (very similar to what is called multi-level marketing), had significant positive effects on many people, spreading exponentially with far-reaching effects, many of which were not revealed until the end of the story.

I mention this concept and the story behind it because I believe that the practice of Servant Leadership principles potentially can have the same effect. However, treating people with Servant Leadership principles has even greater potential because it is not limited to three people. I believe that if we treat people with Servant Leadership principles and let our personal, family, social, and business lives be governed by those principles, we have the opportunity to positively impact the lives of many people and maybe even the world.

The strength of Servant Leadership is that it is not simply a concept, theory, or some clever catch-phrase to be taken lightly. Servant Leadership is based on solid behaviors, actions, and dictums that, in my opinion, we should understand better in order to promote it further. We should strive to improve our own use of these principles.

As I hope you understand, I am not implying that Servant Leadership principles were not being used or practiced before Robert Greenleaf coined the phrase in 1970. However, I do not think that in previous generations we spent as much time identifying and thinking about how people became successful in their given careers.

I would suggest that the practice of Servant Leadership principles and characteristics was a commonplace even many years ago, but we did not recognize it, understand it, or give it a name. As I wrote earlier, it was very beneficial for me to see my father consummate and agree upon contracts with his neighbors by shaking hands.

Unfortunately, that practice has all but disappeared, replaced by attorneys and long, often incomprehensible documents that require interpretation by another battery of lawyers. Modern corporate business practices make many of us long for the behaviors that I observed as a child.

Those characteristics and principles observed then have now been given a name, and that name is Servant Leadership. They carry the same kind of significance and importance as they did many years ago, perhaps even more so in a world that grows increasingly complex and self-centered.

And now that we have given those principles a definition and description of how they can be applied, we need to look at their implementation in our daily lives. I truly believe that success is the positive result of practicing Servant Leadership.

Signposts of Success

One of the premises that I am assuming is that the proper application and use of Servant Leadership principles in your life will ultimately transfer to success. Although Servant Leadership principles can be applied to any profession, career, or life, I have chosen to look into the areas of education, business, healthcare, politics, athletics, and religion.

Before I go further, let's agree on what we mean by "success."

The dictionary's definition of success is, "the achievement of something desired, planned for, or attempted." What is desired, planned for, or attempted is up to each individual, and would, in most cases, include specific goals. Additionally, the degree of desired success varies a great deal from person to person. For some, owning a home is the pinnacle of success; for others it might be the freedom to travel. Others measure success by peer approval or fame. It is a subjective benchmark. Similarly, I know it would be naïve of me to think that everyone has a goal of becoming a Servant Leader or that success is important to them. However, I do believe it is safe to say that the majority of people who occupy this planet do want to be successful, and that being thought of as a Servant Leader is desirable.

So how do you measure success in education, business, healthcare, politics, athletics, and religion?

When I first thought about that question, I assumed I would just Google for the response I was looking for. That would have been the easy way. But success is subjective and means different things to different people. What determines success in the professions I have chosen to write about is subjective.

In my opinion, there is a direct correlation between the use of Servant Leadership principles and the achievement of success. In an attempt to convince you of this, I will be sharing interviews with people in several professions. I have transcribed their unadulterated responses to my questions. I could editorialize and summarize their comments, but I would rather that you to read their own words.

As I continue this journey of putting thoughts into words, I will share with you my personal beliefs regarding what defines successful Servant Leaders in the fields of education, business, healthcare, politics, athletics, and religion. I will then give a brief introduction of the people I have interviewed. And following the interview itself, I will share my reflections on the interview. At the end of each interview, I offer some contemplative questions that emerged from the interview, asking you to focus on those questions yourself.

I encourage you to use this book as a roadmap for the things you wish to achieve in life.

Please start your engines. Here we go!

Servant Leadership
in EDUCATION

What Is a Successful Leader in Eduation?

In education there are obvious tests and measurements that educators can point to in defining success. From kindergarten through high school, on into college and post graduate work, there are continual objectives. How a teacher's students perform on tests determines, to a certain degree, how successful that teacher is in imparting knowledge to his or her students. That is just one part of success in education.

Another component, in my opinion even more important, is what a student learns about life from his or her teacher. Many of the interviews done for this book reflected upon teachers who served as important role models. The degree to which students learn good values, ethics, and morals from their teachers is a strong measurement of a successful Servant Leader. To have a student come up to you later in life and communicate the important positive role you played in his or her life must be very rewarding.

Successfully progressing students through the prescribed curriculum from the beginning of the school-year to the end is a measurable goal.

How those students retain what has been taught and whether or not they see their teacher as a positive role model in their life is also what determines success.

And, of course, the success of those educators who desire to move into administrative roles is determined by how well they communicate their visionary ideas for that school or that district, and how well they do at getting their subordinates to follow them.

I believe you will decide that the people I interviewed in the area of education achieved their desired goal, and that they are, indeed, successful Servant Leaders.

JERRY KEMBER

Education is certainly an arena that we hope is the home to many Servant Leaders. Teachers have the opportunity to positively influence our young people more than any other segment of our society. I was intent on interviewing someone who exemplified Servant Leadership in education, and the name Jerry Kember immediately came to mind. Even though I barely knew Jerry on a personal basis, I was aware of how respected he was within the school district he served as Superintendent, and within the community in which he lived.

Jerry was named the Wisconsin State Superintendent of the Year in 2010 and was given the highly prestigious Community Service Award by the La Crosse Chamber of Commerce in 2011. In that same year he was selected to be Festmaster for the La Crosse Oktoberfest.

Prior to his entrance into administration, Jerry was a music and band instructor. He was happy to share his view on the importance of Servant Leadership in our school systems.

Let's Meet Jerry Kember

GB: Jerry, let's begin this interview by your sharing what the concept of Servant Leadership means to you?

JERRY: It's simply about respecting and valuing beliefs, ideas, and values of other people. To me, that captures it all. It sounds simplistic to talk about respect, but respect comes at so many different levels. Some leaders think they have all the answers and they know what's best, but that's simply not the case.

One thing I've learned about leadership is not to answer questions specifically. You get to these places in your career, and you think you know. Particularly in education, you may think if you're a teacher, you can influence a classroom; if you're a principal, you can influence a school; and so on and so forth. You believe if you could be superintendent, as an example, it's an empowering thing to think that you could have an influence over and make things happen for more people. But the reality is, you find out that the further you go on any of those career tracks, that you are also servant to more people. And so, to be honest with you, I think the further you go on your career track, your opportunity to have it your way becomes less, not greater, because you are responding and trying to be so respectful of so many. Your ideas actually become subservient to everybody else's.

GB: Do you feel or sense that you have a responsibility to help people see what your way is or things as you see them?

JERRY: I call it planting seeds. First, you plant a seed. Sometimes you plant a seed or an idea, and sometimes it gets no reaction initially at all or no response or no interest. And then years later, someone else will bring to the table that seed or idea you planted two or three years ago, and you go, "Yeah, let's do that. Let's go there." And they're excited. Now it's their idea, which is great, because I could care less about whose idea it is. I care more about whether or not it works. So it's fun to see that. I've seen that happen a number of times. Sometimes you have to let things nurture and grow. It takes time, so you try not to be impatient.

GB: I have to believe you are a Servant Leader in your personal and professional life. Do you think of yourself as a Servant Leader?

JERRY: I think it's more of a goal for me. I don't think you ever arrive. I think it's something you're always working toward. I probably haven't been a very good Servant Leader in some aspects of my life, but what's great about Servant Leadership is that it can apply to all aspects of your life. I don't think it's somewhere you arrive. I think it's always something you're trying to get better at. It's hard work. And you catch yourself, as you come to know more about what Servant Leadership is, you catch yourself saying, "Hey, wait a minute, that's not good Servant Leadership—back off." And so I don't think there's any point in time where you think you've arrived.

If you take the two words by themselves and if you go back fifty years, people probably would have said those two words don't go together. Servant? Leader? But we've come to learn over time that we are able to do so much more when we respect and value the opinions and beliefs of others.

My background is music, so when I started in high school and then college, I thought of the famous conductors in music. Fifty years ago, the conductor knew the best way. The attitude was that you just do what the conductor says. There was no involvement other than you do what the conductor tells you. And that worked for a long time and as a result developed some beautiful, phenomenal orchestras. Look back at Toscanini and some of these famous names. But what the new conductors have learned is that when you bring in the opinions and ideas of the whole ensemble, you'll take it to another level. There's somewhat of a lid on it when the conductor says, "This is what we're going to do. Your idea doesn't count. My idea counts. I'm the conductor." Today's best orchestras don't operate that way. They are continually taking in others' ideas and what everyone has to offer to the organization. And that's true of Servant Leadership. Good Servant Leadership is about unleashing the talent of everyone. They could get to this level with the other style, but what we've come to learn is that there's so much farther to go if you unleash the talent of everyone.

GB: How would you say Servant Leadership principles have benefited you and others around you?

JERRY: I would hope that others feel that we're in a system where everyone can freely offer their ideas and their talents, and that they are recognized as important. I've never been into bureaucracy. I've never been into who supervises whom. It's true that there are times in any organization when somebody has to make the final decision.

Any idea I've ever had, when taken to a group, discussed, and fleshed out, has always been improved. The whole is greater than the sum of the parts. It takes all of us. "We're all in this together" is a model I've tried to employ so that people feel that they are a positive and important contributing member of the organization. It doesn't matter what position they have. Everyone can contribute and needs to contribute, and then they feel valued.

GB: Do you feel that someone is a servant first and then becomes a leader, or vice versa?

JERRY: I think when you model and apply the behaviors that you want from others, when you share the gifts and the talents that you have, and when you do it with dedication and passion, that is what makes you a leader. Anybody can do that. It doesn't matter what your position is. If they can show the dedication they have, share the passion they have, share the talents they have in whatever role they have, then they are a leader. We have leaders among our cooks, we have leaders among our teachers, and we have leaders among our custodians—because they are dedicated professionals who have great talents. They perform their duties with passion, energy, and dedication. That inspires me. It's awesome. And it has nothing to do with position or authority. It isn't about that at all. It's about who you are as a person and how you conduct yourself.

GB: What person or persons that you viewed as Servant Leaders have had a positive impact on your life?

JERRY: I don't know where I would start. I am influenced by so many people every day in so many ways, and those people influence my attitude and my own behaviors all the time. I think life's a journey, and we're all shaped by those experiences. It's those experiences and the people who enter into those experiences with us that influence us all the time. Have I had people that I've admired? Absolutely. My high school band director, several teachers along the way, other administrators that I've worked with. I don't think a day goes by that I don't see something or hear something that influences me as to who I am and how I behave.

GB: Obviously, as a leader of a large organization, you have experienced negative conflicts. It's impossible not to. How do you feel you have used Servant Leadership principles in the resolution of those conflicts?

JERRY: We've all had personal conflicts. I don't know anybody who doesn't as they go through life.

But those conflicts stretch your thinking, challenge your beliefs, and help you grow as an individual. And it also grows your understanding of how others think, act, and behave. We really need to be respectful of that. You have to walk in someone else's shoes for awhile to really understand where they're coming from. So personal conflicts—while no one welcomes them—I can't think of one that hasn't made me grow as a result. It's sometimes during the hardest moments that we learn the greatest lessons. We don't want to have them too often, because when you're in the heat of it, it doesn't feel like a lot of fun, but if you can look back later and say, "Well, what did I learn from that? How did I grow? Has it made me think in a different way? Do I understand something better?"

GB: Do you believe that Servant Leadership principles can be taught, learned, or both?

JERRY: Well, teaching and learning are totally different. I think the concept can be taught, but the only way we'll know if the concepts were learned is when that individual can demonstrate or apply it. Through experience, we demonstrate what we've learned. This happens all the time in education. A teacher may think they provided the greatest lesson and experience for the kids, and then they get the tests back and find out they didn't get it. And I'm not talking about simply regurgitating facts. I'm talking about the fact that you taught a concept and now you've given them the chance to apply that concept and they can't. The real measure of whether it's been learned comes with experience and if the person can demonstrate that in their own life's experiences. Then you'll know if it worked.

GB: Have you had role models in your life that you've tried to emulate?

JERRY: Sometimes when I get really down on whatever is going on in my office, I tell my administrators I have to get out of the office and get a "kid fix." There's never a time when I visit my schools when those kids don't inspire me. Maybe it's something they say to me or something as simple as me saying "hello" to a student in the hallway. This next generation, you'll love them. This is the next great generation. I can go down the hallway today and say ,"Hi, how are you doing?" "I'm doing great, how are you doing, Mr. Kember?" And that's the level of children today. Our kids today are volunteering, giving back, and doing more than my generation. I think my generation, quite frankly, has been a selfish generation. The Baby Boomers have been selfish, and I think the selfishness continues. I do not see this in the next generation.

I think we're doing a better job of teaching. I think we're teaching values that we didn't before. You know, we stuck to the reading, writing, and arithmetic. We now teach core values—our kids know what our core values are: things like compassion, giving, responsibility, honesty, respect, and perseverance. We have seven core values in our school system. How do you expect a child to turn in an assignment without teaching about responsibility? Completing your homework, completing a project that's due? How do you get students to work together on a team, on a cooperative learning project, without teaching respect for each other? I try to get the message out to our community how much these students give back, because sometimes I think our community feels, with taxes and referendums and everything, that they give, give, give, to the schools, and, of course, they do. They're very generous. At the same time, I like to remind them how much our kids give back.

GB: My last question is, if you could teach young people one thing, what would it be?

JERRY: If I could, I would teach every child how to believe in themselves, know what their talents and abilities are, and how they can use those talents and abilities as a gift to benefit other people. Wouldn't that be a wonderful world? I believe that we all come into this world—I don't care what your condition in life is—with some talents and abilities; and as educators, it should be our goal to help them discover what they are and bring them out. When I see a students who lacks belief and confidence in themselves, I just know we haven't done our job. Everybody's got ability and talent, and our goal is to help them find what those are and then how they can you use them in a positive way to benefit other people. When you've done that, then you know you have done your job well.

Reflections

It was evident in my conversation with Jerry that he has a passion for education and, more importantly, for students. He actively practices Servant Leadership principles by putting the needs and concerns of others first. I found it particularly interesting to hear how he believes in and promotes the policy that the solution or resolution of problems oftentimes exists within the people for whom you're trying to solve the problem. I witnessed the excitement in Jerry's voice and the light in his eyes when he talked about seeing his students present wise, thoughtful, and mature methods to solve or prevent problems.

A true Servant Leadership principle in education is to feel and demonstrate respect for the students. If you are an educator and you want to use Servant Leadership principles, this is a must. How you accomplish it is up to you. Hopefully it is natural for you, but if not, I encourage you to cultivate that feeling of respect.

Along with respect for students is sharing respect for your subordinates and peers. After all, you are all in the job together, the ultimate teamwork concept. Acceptance of and appreciation for their efforts goes a long way toward helping you achieve mutual goals. It was apparent to me that Jerry has a great deal of respect for both students and his colleagues.

Following the interview, Jerry looked up a quote that he referred to from Albert Einstein: "Setting a good example is not the main means of influencing others . . . it is the only means." It could not be said any better! If you were building a Wall of Fame of Servant Leadership principles, that one sentence belongs very close to the top. Jerry has demonstrated in his personal and professional life that he is now and continues to be a good role model.

To Think About

• Do you set a good example for others? Think about how you do or how you can.

• Do you show respect for others?

RICK ARTMAN

Rick Artman began his educational career by receiving an undergraduate degree in psychology at the University of Miami in 1970. He furthered his education by receiving a master's degree in education in 1972 and a doctorate at the same university in 1979.

He has held many positions in the area of education, ranging from Dean of Students, assistant to the Vice President, and Vice President at three different universities. He served as President of Sienna Heights University from 1994 to 2006. In 2006, he was selected to serve as President of Viterbo University and continues to serve in that capacity.

While pursuing his professional goals, he also spent a lot of time in the classroom. In an effort to maintain contact with students, he continues to teach a class on Franciscan Values and Traditions.

Recognizing the significance of being involved in his community, Rick serves on the boards of many associations and organizations. Additionally, he volunteers his time and talent to numerous community organizations.

Rick has been married to his wife Joan for forty-two years, has two adult married children, and is grandfather to four.

Let's Meet Rick Artman

GB: Rick, first of all I want to know what your understanding is of Servant Leadership.

RICK: For me, it's a paradigm shift from the hierarchal model of leadership. It's not necessarily unique to Servant Leadership, but I think in the last twenty years the literature and research on leadership has shifted from command and control to relational. For me, that shift to leadership as relational is a gift. It's a gift that others give us—to allow us to serve them, to lead them, to lead their organizations. I'm privileged that people here at Viterbo have the trust in me, have the confidence in me to allow me to serve them by leading their organization. It's not an entitlement; it's a gift.

GB: Has this change, this transition from "do it my way" to "what do you think?" been a number of years in the making?

RICK: I think there's a better understanding of what empowers people, and probably it's related to our transition from an agricultural culture to a manufacturing culture to a service industry culture, where in order to get the most out of our employees we need to empower them and enable them to use their skills and talents as opposed to telling them or pushing them. It's a whole different way of thinking, and as people become more educated about leadership, I think there's been a shift. Servant leadership—that concept—is one movement, one element in it, but there are others.

GB: Rick, I chose you for this interview because I see you as a servant leader. Do you see yourself that way?

RICK: Humbly, I do. There are a lot of Christian values in the Servant Leadership movement or practice, and I think in large part it is a good alignment with my faith. In my faith, we have a larger purpose in life, a higher purpose. In Franciscan spirituality, everything is a gift from the Creator, both personal gifts as well as every creature around us. So if some of us are blessed with this gift to have leadership skills and the ability to apply those skills effectively, then I think, "Okay, I've been called to lead," and as I said earlier, it's a gift, a big responsibility to do that. So I think, particularly in the presidency, it's been more clearly defined for me than it was as vice-president or dean of students. You're at a different level, and you really have to start thinking, "what is my purpose, and how can I shape an organization for the betterment of our students and our employees?"

GB: In a lot of ways you've answered my next question, but could you expand a little more on how practicing Servant Leadership principles has benefited you and those around you.

RICK: For me, the Prayer of St. Francis fits so well with the concept of servant leadership—to be an instrument of peace, to bring joy, to bring comfort, to make a difference, and to provide hope instead of despair. All the elements that are in that prayer are great solace for me and a guiding point, because it's actuarian, too. It's not just, "be nice to everybody." I have to get results. The Board expects results. I can be really nice, but if I don't get results, you're going to get another President. If I can't raise money, if I can't have good relationships with the faculty, you'll find someone who will.

It's not that Servant Leadership is soft. There's a high degree of accountability involved. You are obligated to hold people accountable for the betterment of the organization or the community or the family. By not holding people accountable, you are betraying what the servant leader ought to do. It's unjust not to hold people accountable. But then I also think about how do you give employees a sense of value?

Some ways to do that are simple. For example, I make calls on their birthdays. I have a list everyday of people's birthdays. The first thing I do each morning is make my happy birthday calls. It's not a big thing, but it is amazing how that makes people feel. "Wow, the president took time to wish me happy birthday." And it's not because it's a call from Rick Artman; it's a call from the president of their organization that says, "I'm a person, I'm recognized."

And so the stress that people feel here—at least I hope this is the case—is self-imposed, because they believe in our mission. They want to live our values, and they work their tails off. I try to create an environment that allows them to be themselves, to authentically be a part of an organization that has integrity, so they're not worrying about covering their backside all the time, so they know they have the freedom to make a mistake, that they know there are values that guide the organization, rather than whims or self-aggrandizement of the people in power. I think that's how people benefit from my leadership style. It's an environment that, hopefully, allows them to fulfill their potential. We're helping to meet their basic human needs and allowing their talents to be used to the extent that they can make a difference to students.

GB: Do you think that people become leaders first and then Servant Leaders, or become Servant Leaders first and then leaders?

RICK: I don't think one comes before the other. We're the product of all our interactions and all our relationships. I think there are certain skills that people are predisposed to have. You see all kinds of leaders, all stripes—I've had mentors who have been very soft-spoken; I've had mentors who have been very charismatic. And they've all been effective leaders, because they lead authentically within their own character and values. I think leadership is a journey. I'm constantly learning. I read a lot, try to watch other people. So I don't think it's something you're christened with—"you're the leader, now be a Servant Leader." I think you learn, "I'm more effective when my relationships are based on trust rather than on power, when I can model the behaviors that I want to see followed in this organization or that I want my grandchildren to see." It's kind of a yin and a yang. It's back and forth. I don't think you get there linearly.

GB: The main premise of this book, and one of my goals, is that I would like to believe that the more we talk about Servant Leadership, the more we inform people about Servant Leadership and what it is, the more people will strive to become Servant Leaders. Servant Leadership is a term given now to characteristics and personalities that have existed forever, but I think if we define the term and talk about more, people will aspire to become Servant Leaders. Would you agree?

RICK: I think so. But you don't want to get hung up on the term, either. You can't think, "I can be a Servant Leader by doing these things, by finding these things." Effective leadership has to be authentic. People won't follow you, they won't extend their faith and confidence in you, if they don't have trust in you, and so it's really that leadership is relational, not hierarchal. We earn trust; we don't give it to you with a title. You can do a few things as president, but over time if you're using the power of the chair, the position, you're going to run out of steam.

So yes, I think people are beginning to understand there's a new way of leading, and if you call it Servant Leadership, I think that makes sense for me because of the Gospel teaching the importance of service and being called to make a difference in life. And maybe people begin thinking, "Well, I can be a Servant Leader in my family, I can be a Servant Leader in my community, if I serve on the school board, etc." We can serve in many different ways, and leadership comes and goes. You and I are followers in some groups; we're leaders in others. So you go back and forth, and a good Servant Leader is a good follower, too.

GB: Do you think that someone who presently is not a Servant Leader can develop the characteristics of Servant Leadership?

RICK: Yes, I do. I think authenticity is the key here. If you're doing it because you read it in a book and think this will work, it's like taking the latest fad and trying to implement managerial or leadership fads. If it's not your gift, it will become transparent eventually to people around you. But, yes, I do believe leadership has a learned dimension to it. I've taught leadership courses on campus, believing that if we can devote the time, students can learn more effective leadership skills. Like playing tennis or racquetball or basketball or piano—you have to practice it, and if you don't practice it, you aren't going to get better. So people can say, "Well, that Servant Leadership sounds pretty good to me, and I'll do those things," but if they don't really bring it into their life and all their relationships, it's not going to work for them. If they think, "Oh, I can do this if I'm a Servant

Leader, people will respond better to me," they may not succeed, because people see through it. If you just don't have the perseverance to change the way you do things, it won't work. We also know people learn by watching. If we talk about Servant Leadership here at the University and our behaviors don't model those principles, our students will know it.

GB: You obviously don't get to the position you have and stay there without having some conflicts. How do you think you employ Servant Leadership principles in the resolution of those conflicts?

RICK: That's a really tough question, because in leadership it's often personnel issues you deal with, and those are the thorniest and toughest. It's a vulnerability to those of us who strive to follow a Servant Leadership model, because you care about your people. It's hard to make the necessary decisions for an organization when a livelihood is at stake, a family is at stake. A conflict of ideas is easy to resolve. You just agree to disagree, and you move on because we're all different. But a conflict over behavior is more difficult. How can you do what's best for the organization if you don't deal with it? Ultimately, you have to deal with it.

I think with the Servant Leadership model, you

care enough about the person, you coax them, you try to enable them to be successful. My experience has been that all those people I've had to terminate, they knew it ahead of time. It wasn't a surprise. They had it in writing—they were told you need to improve, you need to change—but he or she didn't quite get it. In almost all those cases, they went on to do other things where they were more successful. It was just a bad match for what was needed at the time for that organization and what the skills and talents were that they had to give. Sometimes it takes tough love. You need to praise, but you also need to hold people accountable. Praising is a good habit, and it's a lot easier than telling someone they're not measuring up. But if you have integrity, you have to do that, too, especially if you're entrusted with leadership. And it isn't easy. It has never gotten easier, and I don't think it ever will.

GB: Have you or do you have role models in your life that you try to emulate?

RICK: Sure. I also had one supervisor in my career from whom I learned what not to do. A reverse role model. You learn from mentors what to do, and you also learn what not to do. You're always in that learning mode. The three people who have influenced me the most would include two college presidents in relation to my professional life, and the third would be my wife, Joan, who has been a wonderful influence on me. She is my center, my core; she keeps me grounded. The three all have different styles, and that has convinced me to respect the various people who I select to be part of my team. People who complement me.

GB: What is the most important thing that you would like to tell young people about how to become successful leaders?

RICK: That leadership is relational; it's built on trust like all relationships. Trust is earned, not given in a title, and if it's lost, it's tough to restore it. What we have ultimately is our character and our integrity, and if we stray from that, it will diminish our effectiveness. Like all success in life, it's relational. Working in sales is relational. Military is relational. As hierarchal as the military is, guys don't jump on a hand grenade because of rank or a bill that might be in Congress. They jump on it because of the guy next to them, someone they trained with and that they love and care about. I really think that's what young people have to understand. So how do you build relationships? It's back to those core principles, values, having a moral compass about you, being dependable. Those are the things we need to teach young people.

Reflections

I found my interview with Rick to be insightful and filled with original thoughts. His thoughts about Servant Leadership being a transition from command-and-control to a leader gaining leadership through relations was profound. As he says, "This is a paradigm shift." Most people understand that those in leadership roles want their subordinates to follow. The likelihood of achieving that goal is more rewarding and gratifying if achieved through positive relational behaviors.

It was intriguing to hear Rick explain how he draws a comparison and correlation to the alignment of his Christian faith to that of a Servant Leader. Prior to Rick's statement about that, I had not concluded that in my own self-understanding. After being introduced to the comparison, it is easy for me to concur.

While it was obvious that Rick would do most anything to avoid conflict with staff and employees, he understands that, as a true leader, it would be unjust not to hold people accountable for their less-than-acceptable performance. As a Servant Leader, he is devoted to making every attempt to correct on-going or potential conflicts. He realizes that it would be a detriment to his organization and all the people that are a part of that organization not to resolve conflicts or ultimately implement termination procedures.

According to Rick, it is not a question of whether you become a leader first and then a Servant Leader, or vice versa. He explains that this is not a linear process; one does not come before or after the other. Rather, they emerge and grow together, and the authenticity of both must be present to be successful as a Servant Leader.

To Think About

• Do components of your faith coincide with your Servant Leadership characteristics?

• Do you use relational qualities or controlling qualities when you try to lead?

DARRYLE CLOTT

For my next stop along the way, I arrived at the home of Darryle Clott. I have known Darryle for over thirty years. She was the English and social studies teacher for all four of my children, and they always enjoyed her classes and her enthusiasm, remarking on how enjoyable, informative, and positive she was.

Darryle taught in the La Crescent, Minnesota, high school for many years before retiring, and she now serves as an adjunct teacher at Viterbo University, focusing on informing and educating students about the Holocaust. Her work has been recognized internationally, and she has been recipient of many prestigious awards for her efforts. Most recently, she was honored with the Ellis Island Medal of Honor, presented to individuals who have excelled in humanitarian efforts. By anyone's measurement, Darryle's life has been a success.

Let's Meet Darryle Clott

GB: Darryle, what is your understanding of Servant Leadership?

DARRYLE: To serve others—to lead by serving others. A good friend of mine defines Servant Leadership as co-creating a culture of goodness. I like that definition.

GB: I chose you for this interview because I have seen you practice Servant Leadership in your personal and professional life. Have you thought of yourself as a Servant Leader?

DARRYLE: I had never heard the term Servant Leadership until a few years ago. Until then, I never thought about it. Once I heard about it, I realized that I have been a Servant Leader all along.

GB: That's interesting. Now that you recognize yourself as a Servant Leader, do you believe that has benefited other people around you?

DARRYLE: Yes, as a teacher I cared greatly about my students, encouraging them to learn all they can and become all they can. From the brightest to those with far less gifts, I always tried to teach them a great deal more than just subject manner. Part of that means teaching them to do the best job, no matter what the job is.

I was also the forensics (public speaking) coach. Each year I required all students to give four speeches. I knew if students could speak in front of a group, they would gain confidence and thus leadership skills. I would pick out students who had the potential to be good public speakers and encourage them to go out for forensics. Often they were quiet students who just needed encouragement. They needed someone to believe in them. Because they knew I believed in them, they would blossom and grow

I have benefited greatly from being a Servant Leader because I reap the rewards of seeing my students work to their potential. I have the very best job on the face of the earth, because I get to watch them grow into young adults.

GB: You are a successful leader in your role and discipline in life. Do you think a successful person becomes a leader first and then develops an attitude of serving, or vice versa?

DARRYLE: I am not sure. It is a little like what came first, the chicken or the egg. In my own life I have been greatly influenced by the fact that I am the oldest of six children. My mother was a nurse who worked full time. My father worked construction and was frequently away; therefore, I ended up helping raise my three sisters, who are ten, eleven, and twelve years younger than me. This definitely made me a servant, but it also prepared me for leadership roles which I have assumed all my life. I know leaders who are servants and servants who are not leaders. I think a successful person who becomes a leader is probably a servant first. This is especially true in teaching.

Teachers are servants. We constantly serve our students. Kids know the teachers who really care. In order to be an effective teacher, we must gain our students trust. They need to know that we have their best interest in mind. I believe that a good teacher can teach any student if one cares enough. Teaching is not always an easy profession, if one really cares about students and learning. It can be all-consuming. However, as I said before, it is the best job on the face of the earth.

GB: What person or persons in your life have had the most influence on you in becoming the person you are today?

DARRYLE: First of all, I would say my parents. My mother was a true Servant Leader. She was a head nurse in the little town where I went to high school. I watched my mother. She had a great reputation at the hospital. She was an excellent nurse, and I heard it everywhere I went. And not only was she a nurse at the hospital, but she was a nurse in our neighborhood. If anyone was sick, Mom would get a call—so I grew up watching her serve. She lived to serve people. She was a great cook, and she loved to feed people. She lived to serve and to feed people. You can't help but be influenced by that.

Another thing that I credit my mother with is my positive thinking. And here's why. You know kids like to complain, and I'd come home from school and I'd complain about someone, and she'd listen, and then she'd say, "Okay, now tell me something good about that person." And it got to the point where it wasn't worth coming home and complaining about anyone. Pretty soon I was only looking at the good in others. I really think my mother is the one to whom I would have to attribute my positive thinking. My mother tried to do three good deeds every day of her life. She set out on purpose—it wasn't just by chance. She purposely tried to do three good deeds a day, whether it was baking something and taking it to someone she thought needed it, whether it was making a phone call to someone, or whether it was dropping a note to somebody, etc.

My father also had a strong influence on me. He was such an honest man. He taught us to never to take advantage of anyone. My dad always went for the underdog. I can remember one time my parents had this local person do their taxes. He sent their bill in the mail, and my dad didn't think that he had charged them enough. So when my dad wrote the check out to send it to him, he added $25 to the check. Back then, $25 was a pretty good amount of money. I have always remembered that, not to take advantage of people, to give what is fair, to be fair.

GB: And just think of the impact that simple act had on you.

DARRYLE: I know. I feel so blessed. My dad was a great listener. He listened to us, and he always encouraged me to follow my dreams. No matter what I wanted to do, no matter what I thought of attempting, he'd always say, "Darryle, no guts, no glory."

I have had many other people who have also served as role models to me from many different walks of life.

GB: In every walk of life, people who are successful in what they do have also had conflicts in their life. And so my question is, how do you feel you have used Servant Leadership principles in dealing with conflict?

DARRYLE: You know, I think kindness. When I had a student that I had an issue or issues with, I would love them to death. I think kindness can work miracles. I remember a student I had in class who was belligerent, acted tough, and was a bad influence on the other kids. I started dealing with him by butting heads, and then I had an unbelievable experience. Because of his disruptive behavior, the guidance counselor coordinated a meeting to discuss his problems. They needed a teacher to sit in on a meeting along with the guidance counselor, and the mother was supposed to be at this meeting, as well. They needed a teacher who had this boy in class, so I got the job. I went in there with a real chip on my shoulder about this kid. First, the guidance counselor talked about him and about his horrible family situation. His mother had him when she was fifteen. When she came in late, she walked in with white go-go boots and a little mini-skirt and then talked about her son in the worst tone you can imagine.

When I walked out of that meeting, I was a changed teacher. I went back into my room and had this student the next hour. I went from butting heads with him to loving him to death. For the rest of the year, two hours a day, I just loved that kid to death. I encouraged him to write, and I gave him as much praise as I could. I had him read his poetry to the class. He and I ended up having a really strong relationship.

.

GB: Do you think he sensed what you were doing?

DARRYLE: I don't think he knew why I was doing it, but I don't think he had very many people who loved him. I really learned a lot from that experience.

GB: So because you saw the way his mother saw him and felt toward him, you thought he needed love.

DARRYLE: Absolutely. And what better person to give him love than his teacher? I saw him every single day, and he blossomed. I took it upon myself to try to help my students feel good about themselves.

GB: That's a real gift.

DARRYLE: It's a gift to me to be able to do that, because some of them just didn't have anybody to help them feel good about themselves.

GB: These weren't just people who sat behind a desk to you.

DARRYLE: No! One time the science teacher said to me, "Darryle, the only difference between you and me is that you never give up on these kids."

GB: That is another Servant Leadership princi-ple—to never give up. Do you think Servant Leadership principles are taught or learned or both?

DARRYLE: Both. Sometimes we teach them by modeling them. My senior high school teacher used to have a saying—"You can preach a better sermon with your life than your words." And it's so true.

GB: So there again, you saw your teacher do that, and it had a positive influence on you, and you wanted to emulate that.

DARRYLE: It's true. She was a really tough English teacher. She devoted her whole life to teaching, and a lot of the things I did as an English teacher came from watching her. You have to have high expectations. I never watered things down. You can be tough, but you can still show love.

I had a college professor that was a true gentleman. He taught me to get things done gracefully. I think that's something that I had to learn, because, if you go in there like a bull in a china shop and try to do things by force, it doesn't work. You have to get people to join you willingly, and I think he taught me how to get things done gracefully.

He modeled it. He was such a gentleman—a gentle person—he really had an influence on me, because he got things done, but they were not forced down our throats. I had to learn that, because I had to be so responsible at home and had to make my siblings follow rules.

GB: Last question, Darryle. If you could teach young people one thing and one thing only, what would it be?

DARRYLE: The importance of having a positive attitude, absolutely, bar none. Because your attitude is the way you act, think, and feel, I would teach my kids that we own our attitudes, and if we don't think our attitude is getting us anywhere, we have the ability to change it. We are the only ones who have the power to change that. I cannot imagine why anybody would want to waste their time on negative thinking. You can look at something positively or negatively. Why would you want to waste time on negative thinking? If possible, I try not to hang out with negative people.

Reflections

The answers Darryle gave to my questions cannot possibly convey the enthusiasm in her voice and gestures as she spoke. Compassion and passion were the overwhelming themes of this interview. She had not identified herself as a Servant Leader until a few years ago, simply because she was not familiar with or aware of the concept. Since she has learned about what Servant Leadership means, she now realizes that she possessed many of the characteristics of Servant Leadership most of her life. I found it interesting and amazing to see how happy she is to be a Servant Leader. Enjoying the opportunity to serve and teach others is at the very core of who she is. She still possesses the same kind of enthusiasm about what she does that I observed thirty years ago. In my opinion, she exemplifies the type of teacher you would want your children to have in the classroom.

Her philosophy that ordinary people can accomplish extraordinary things if only they have a passion and a dream and are willing to work hard to make that dream come true, should be an inspiration to everyone. I strongly believe in this philosophy as well, and I encourage everyone to work at making that passion a part of their lives. Darryle and I both agree that encouraging and motivating others to be the best they can be is a vital component of being a Servant Leader.

To Think About

• Do you encourage and motivate others?

• Do you love what you do?

Servant Leadership
in BUSINESS

What Is a Successful Leader in Business?

What determines success in business is easier for me to comment on, having been in business for so many years myself. I was fortunate to be able to start several businesses and have them become successful in terms of sustainability and growth. I think many people who have never owned a business have an unclear idea of what obtaining success in business entails.

Success in business should not just be measured by the amount of money generated. Of course, financial success is important, but how a business owner makes his or her business financially successful is more important. Just as earning and maintaining the loyalty and respect of employees is a key component, earning the respect and trust of customers is the most successful way of improving and growing the bottom line. Servant Leadership principles go a long way in forging strong relationships between customers and employees, owners and management, and vendors and management.

I always enjoyed going to work because I viewed

my associates (employees) as friends. And as friends, I cared about what was happening in their personal lives, and they cared about the important things that were occurring in my life.

I believe that success in business should be measured by how much the employees feel they are contributing to or benefiting from the success of the company for which they work. Respecting their ideas, listening to their concerns, and giving them the chance to actively contribute to the operation of the company can help build and maintain a successful business.

Customer satisfaction is what really propels a company's financial success. How much attention is given to customers ultimately determines business success.

A business owner has everything to do with setting the tone and atmosphere of the business culture. It is certainly no secret that anyone who decides to take all the risks that go along with starting a business has high hopes of achieving financial success. It is also no secret that the majority of new business ventures are not successful. I believe that the risk-takers who practice Servant Leadership principles have the greatest potential for overcoming the odds.

DON WEBER

If you happen to live in the La Crosse, Wisconsin, community and you have not heard the name Don Weber, you must be living in a cave. The term "pillar of the community" is often over-used, but in Don's case it is most deserved, not only for the employment opportunities he has brought to the region, but for the philanthropic role he plays in the community.

Don Weber is the company founder and CEO of Logistics Health, Inc. He has twenty-five years of experience in designing and implementing creative health-service programs. His leadership and vision have driven the development of many comprehensive and successful approaches to providing healthcare services to employers and employees alike.

In 2004, Weber was named Wisconsin Entrepreneur of the Year, an award which recognizes entrepreneurial leaders instrumental in the development of the Wisconsin economy. He was also named the *La Crosse Tribune*'s Person of the Year for 2006, and is an active community leader, serving on the boards of the Family and Children's Center, Viterbo University, the Boys and Girls Club of La Crosse, the La Crosse Area Family YMCA, and the Gundersen Lutheran Medical Foundation. He and his wife, Roxie, have received numerous awards and recognition for their philanthropy.

When I thought about someone I wanted to interview about how Servant Leadership principles are applied in business, he was at the top of my list. I was intrigued by the possibility of finding out what propelled him to be a Servant Leader, and how he visualized and applied Servant Leadership principles in his business career and personal life

Let's Meet Don Weber

GB: I have developed a real passion for writing this book, and part of the reason is that I want to expose other people to people I believe have practiced Servant Leadership principles and have become successful. I think I have a pretty good understanding of your philosophy, but a lot of people don't. So one of the things I hope to do by writing this book is to expose others to people like yourself. So my first question is, What is your understanding of Servant Leadership? What does that concept mean to you?

DON: Up until a couple of years ago, I never even thought about it or whether or not I fit into that category. I guess for me it's about serving others. I believe that we serve God by serving others. I believe that a life of service is not first about what you do; it's about who you are. I don't think about myself as though I'm doing this or that because I want the glory and the recognition. No. I think about what will my contribution be to life? God gave us all the gift of life. I believe there is purpose for all of us, and we are all here to make a positive difference in the lives of others. Some of us have a hard time trying to figure out what that purpose is. We all have a mission, and your mission gives your life meaning.

I believe everything we have is a gift and that the gifts we have received are to be used for the service of others. Happiness—it's temporary. But joy lasts forever. Joy comes from the heart, and it comes from giving. Think about life and how short it is—my mom once told me, life here on earth is shorter than the blink of an eye compared with eternity. And that's got to be true. Eternity's forever and ever and ever. So God gave me this little bit of time, and, with that, not only did He give me the gift of life, but everything else I have is a gift. It's to be shared.

I can accumulate things, material things that bring happiness for a while, but not true joy. True joy is when I know that somehow I made a positive difference in someone else's life. Talk about a life of fulfillment, a sense of well-being—you can't buy that.

One of the things that I sometimes struggle with is that God gave me so many gifts, including financial rewards. I don't believe success should ever be measured by your financial worth. I think money has the greatest potential to replace God. It gives you power, and you can abuse it. I don't ever want that to happen. I struggle with that sometimes, I really do. If I don't focus on that thought, I can forget.

GB: Who do you believe has had the most positive influence on you and helped you shape your philosophy of life?

DON: First of all, I would definitely say my mother and father. As a little kid, I really felt sorry for myself. We were poor farmers. My mom and dad struggled and worked seven days a week. We had a lot of chores to do. And yet I always saw them, with what little they had, giving up things and giving their time to others who were struggling even worse than we. And then sometimes I would see them helping people who had a lot more than we had, and I would say to myself, "Wait a minute. What about us?" I felt sorry for myself. We always had a beat-up car, and the neighbors had a new car. The neighbors had a TV, and we didn't have a TV. The neighbors had indoor plumbing and bathrooms, and we had an outhouse.

Yet my parents were always helping out everyone else. There were days after Dad worked really hard and came home tired, he was helping somebody else out. I never could figure that out when I was a kid.

Then I got sent to Vietnam, and it didn't take me any time at all to change my feeling. I was ashamed of how I felt, because now I saw people in really poor conditions. What I had was so much more than they had. I had a father and a mother who were both there for me. There were very few male figures there. They were off fighting wars. They were gone. Or many of them were crippled; many of the families lived in bamboo huts with dirt floors. They didn't have running water; they didn't have electricity. They didn't have healthcare; they didn't have food to eat. They were begging for leftovers. Seeing those things really helped me realize that when I was home and we were having the same thing to eat tonight as last night, or Mom would take old potatoes and make potato soup from the cream off the top of the milk, that I was pretty fortunate.

The Marine Corps turned so much of my life around. People ask if you are born a leader or made a leader? I believe you're made a leader. The Marine Corps made a leader out of me, but it was seeing my Mom and Dad giving back—I think it was a combination of those two things—that instilled in me the person I am today. I watched a little video a few weeks back. It was made when I was inducted into the Boys and Girls Club Wall of Fame. They had interviewed my mom and some other people for this video. She said, "I remember a Christmas when Don was in Vietnam and he sent home $100. He said give $50 to the church and tell them to use it for whatever they need it for." That was a lot of money back then. There were times I would see Mom and Dad scrounge up dimes and nickels to give to the church on Sunday. When Dad smoked and cigarettes were 20 cents a pack, he would drop that 20 cents in the collection box, and then he would go out and look for cigarette butts that hadn't been smoked down. That 20 cents meant as much to him as probably $20 means to me today. But he gave that up, and that is really what giving and serving is all about. It's truly when you are willing to do without. It's when you give something that will make a difference to someone's life. That's giving back.

There is nothing greater than when you can give of your own personal time. The greatest gift is life, and the most precious thing we have is our time. Like my mother told me, in the Bible it says time here on earth is shorter than the blink of an eye compared to eternity, so think of how much time we really have. So when someone gives back of their own personal time, there's no greater love you can show for anyone or anything.

GB: How do you think other people have benefitted from you practicing Servant Leadership?

DON: One of my passions is job creation. I love it. I love to see young people and seniors employed. We have people we hired who have five years left to retire. In order for a community, a region, a state, a country to prosper, people have to have good jobs. After World War II, that is what made this country so great. All the development that went on and all the hard work that went into it and all the blue collar jobs and all the laborers—now so many of those jobs are gone. So it is companies like ours that have to create new forms of employment. So I believe one of my purposes or missions in life is to create jobs, and I enjoy seeing how my efforts have benefitted many people

Last week I was asked to appear at a confirmation hearing in front of the state senate. I told them, "I think you all should come to La Crosse. First of all, it's one of the most beautiful spots in the world; it's gorgeous up there. If you go there, look at the rest of the state, look at the country. Look at unemployment. It's double digits. Other than Madison, there's no other part of the state where unemployment has consistently been under six per cent. And we have been maintaining that. There are cranes in the sky, there is construction going on, hospitals are being built, universities are growing and expanding." And I said "We can take what we have here, and we can mirror this in other parts of the state. It can be done." I really believe that. That's what I get excited about. I hope that by what I do, I can influence others.

GB: It is impossible to become successful in business and to have no conflicts. How do you think you have used Servant Leadership principals to handle conflicts?

DON: I think the action of really listening to people is the key. I have had to learn how to do that, and I am still learning. There have been many times, because of listening to others, I have reversed my opinion. I try to look at people as though they know more about things than I do. You also have to be willing to compromise. Even though you may not agree with their opinion, you have to show them respect by the way you communicate to them.

What is very important to me, and what I have

tried to instill this in my management team, is that when a decision is made, whether you agreed with it or not, when we leave the room, we all support that decision.

GB: You have been the recipient of some negative criticism in the media regarding some of your dealings with the local government. How do you deal with that kind of negativism on a personal basis?

DON: I came across a quote by John Bunyan that says, "If my life is fruitless, it doesn't matter who praises me, and if my life is fruitful, it doesn't matter who criticizes me." Individually, we are the only ones who have to look at ourselves in the mirror in the morning. A lot of times we are our own worst critics. Ultimately, we have to satisfy our own moral and value parameters for our life.

GB: If you could pass on one thing to the next generation what would it be?

DON: I would encourage them to develop an attitude of giving back in proportion to the way they have been blessed. I would also encourage them to never fear failure. I have personally learned a lot from some of my own failures. It is impossible to become successful in life without having experienced failure.

Reflections

You can see by the way Don responded to my questions that he is, without a doubt, a Servant Leader.

Reflecting on my interview with Don was fun and invigorating to do because he offered so much information. The theme of the importance of giving back was one principle that kept coming through. Giving back is at the very center of his philosophy of life. He does not think of giving back just in financial terms, but also by supporting and encouraging others. A key component of giving back for Don is not to give because of the potential recognition, but because of the good that one is able to accomplish. This is the very essence and definition of humility.

Don speaks with obvious fondness and respect about the ethics and virtues that he gleaned from his mom and dad, and it was inspiring. I'm sure that Don's parents did not consciously do the things that they did because they were intentionally trying to teach their son a lesson. They simply lived their lives that way because they thought it was the right thing to do.

It is obvious that Don's faith in God has played an important role in his life. Doing what he thinks God would want him to do serves as the tour guide to his life. I got the feeling that Don thinks that God has written a script for his life and that it is his responsibility to follow it.

Another virtue of Servant Leadership is crediting others for success, and Don is a strong believer in, and implementer of, that concept.

While Don has been able to enjoy the rewards of his financial success, that is not the most important thing to him. Being able to make a positive difference in the lives of other people is what motivates him to do what he does.

To Think About

• Do you think about ways that you can give back?

• Does God serve as a tour guide to you?

• Do you encourage others to be the best that they can be?

JANET STANSFIELD HESS

Janet Stansfield Hess was born and raised in La Crosse and earned her Bachelor's in Business Administration in 1993 from the University of Wisconsin–Madison. She worked in the Twin Cities for a few years in the buying offices of the Dayton Hudson Corporation (now Marshall Field's–Macy's) and married her high-school sweetheart in 1994. In 1995 she decided to pursue her MBA at the University of Washington in Seattle, thinking she might want to become a business ethics professor, capitalizing on her internship experience researching and developing a business ethics textbook while at UW–Madison.

After graduating in 1997, Janet realized the life of a professor was not for her. At that time, her father approached her about moving back to La Crosse to take over Stansfield Vending, the sixty-year-old family business her grandfather started. Janet and her husband, Troy, moved back to La Crosse in 1997 and started a family.

In 2002, Janet's father sold Stansfield Vending to her and her sister Julie, and Janet has been serving as President of the organization since that time. She has been very involved in the community with organizations such as the La Crosse and Eau Claire Chambers of Commerce, Trust Point, The Mathy

Center, Gundersen Lutheran Medical Center, and the YMCA–Pioneering Healthier Communities, just to name a few. She and Troy live in Onalaska and have three daughters.

Let's Meet Janet Stansfield Hess

GB: The first question is a simple one. What is your concept of Servant Leadership?

JANET: I think my first exposure to the concept was years ago when a friend of mine gave me a copy of *The Servant Leader* by James Autry. It was good for me because I had only been running the company for five years, and it validated me and made me feel better about some of the things I was doing and the kind of person I thought I was. I guess it was an "ah-hah" moment for me in that I learned it was okay to be who I was and that you didn't have to be arrogant and in charge and dictatorial to be a good leader.

Up until that point, in those five years, I felt like I probably didn't belong running a company just because of my personality and who I was. I felt like a fish out of water, and I wasn't sure at the time if it was my age or the fact that I was a woman. I worried so much about being incompetent, because I didn't see what I was doing lining up with what I thought a good leader was. And I read that book and thought, "Maybe I've got a chance." All the other leadership books I had read or the things that I thought to be true about a leader were not me. But I didn't know a different way to be. The way I have always been and the way I was raised was just to be pretty humble. If you've read the book, I'm definitely the example of the leader who's fixing a toilet. If you remember it, and I think I have it right, this fellow goes to a leadership retreat and he hopes to meet this famous leader. The man ends up fixing his toilet.

GB: So you felt like you were conducting your life in the manner of a Servant Leader, but you didn't know if those were the kinds of characteristics that would help you become a good Leader.

JANET: Correct

GB: Servant Leaders come in all sorts of packages, and that's what makes writing this book so interesting. I want to try to convey to other people what it means to be a Servant Leader, just like someone gave you that book. Hopefully, there's going to be someone in this book that each reader can identify with. Now, you've already said you did not see yourself as a Servant Leader before. Do you now?

JANET: Yes, I do. And that's still hard for me to say because now that the term is sort of famous, and while it's a good thing to be that way, it's hard for me to even say that. But yes, when I received that book, it made me feel better. Because nothing up to that time had ever validated for me on the exterior that the way I am is okay, and maybe even good.

GB: Maybe no one ever said to you, "Janet, you are a Servant Leader," but I suspect you got validation from the people you were leading.

JANET: Not exactly. When I came back in 1997 to be part of this company, my husband and I just rented an apartment. I thought, "Let me just give this a try. If they all hate me, and I'm not doing a good job, and I'm miserable, and they oust me, we can just go back to Minneapolis." That was the way I came back. I didn't come back guns blazing and saying, "I'm going to be in charge. Here's what I'm going to do, and there's a new sheriff in town." I literally came back hoping to find my way at Stansfield Vending and hoping that the people I have known my entire life who were twenty years older than I was and had known me since I was in diapers, would even let me just be a part of their group and just let me sweep the floors. And no, they never said the words, "Thank you" and "You're doing a good job. You're a good leader. I like following you." They never said that.

GB: Did you feel that?

JANET: You know, again back to humility, I know it was there, and yes, in hindsight I see that the love was there. But when you're in it and you're so nervous about yourself and what you're contributing, you don't see it. At the time, I didn't see it and I didn't feel it. I was just glad to be getting through the day and glad that I was fitting in and adding value and helping people.

GB: In a sense, you were testing the waters. And not just with this company, but for yourself. You apparently had some prerequisites for yourself to determine if this was what you wanted for the rest of your life. Are you getting closer now to those goals?

JANET: Yes, but only recently.

GB: Is there something that tipped the scale for you, that made you feel that now this is the right fit for you?

JANET: The first five years, my father was still

active in the company. He owned the company. The first five years, I was in charge, but he was still really in charge. I was just feeling my way. In 2002 he sold it to Julie and me. Very quickly he was not around, and clearly not leading. I was named president fairly quickly after I started, but in 2002 after my dad left, it was obvious that I was really in charge. So then it took me another five, six, seven years to really understand that I wasn't merely riding on the coattails of my dad. It took me that long to realize that I did have some responsibility for the success of the company, and I hadn't just avoided screwing it up. He sold it to us almost ten years ago, but only recently have I felt like I am now personally responsible for some of this, probably in the last three years. It's taken me twelve years, but I'm there now.

GB: Do you think that because you now recognize yourself as a Servant Leader, it has helped you reach the point that you now feel comfortable in saying, "Yes, I have made a significant contribution to this company?" How do those Servant Leadership principles that you demonstrate help you to become a successful leader?

JANET: It gives you confidence in yourself and gives you more courage to take it further. Knowing that it is something that books are written about and that it is recognized as a good way to behave as a leader has given me the confidence to make better decisions. You know, the downside of humility is that it can be debilitating. At some point, if you don't have self-confidence and you're not able to hold other people accountable, you risk becoming a doormat. That's one of my weaknesses. I can be a doormat. I can let other people get away with things because I am so humble that I don't have enough self-confidence to hold them accountable for their actions. I'll compensate for their inabilities.

GB: Do you think that you become a leader first and then demonstrate Servant Leadership principles, or vice versa?

JANET: I have trouble with that question because it can go either way. I don't think it's one way or another. I think in my situation it would have been impossible for me to have become any other kind of leader because of my personality and the way I was raised. There was no way I was going to be able to change myself enough to become the type of leader I had read about in other books. So in that way, my personality came first, and then I learned leadership skills. But I still think it can be taught. I don't think you either have it or you don't. I think a person can learn the skills, can be groomed to some extent.

There are, of course, some people who simply are not going to be Servant Leaders. Not everybody can become a good leader—period. I sincerely believe there is no one good leader, one person, or way of leading that is the best. Whatever umbrella you end up putting Servant Leaders under, you will find all different kinds of stories. .

I get something out of every leadership book I read, but this one on Servant Leadership is truest to who I am. This style fits me the best, and it lets me know that I didn't have to change to be successful, that I could do both things at the same time. I think leadership styles have changed over the years—but I think Servant Leadership principles and styles will help take companies into the future. Because people respond to it. But it cannot be faked. There are other books you can read and fake the style. But Servant Leadership is pretty hard to fake.

GB: Who have been the most influential people in your life?

JANET: Both of my parents. My mom never worked in the business, technically, but she influenced me the most. Also an officer here who has worked for us for forty years has positively affected me a lot through-out the years.

GB: You cannot be the president of a company and not have conflicts. Can you relate any ways in which your use of Servant Leadership principles has helped you in resolving conflicts?

JANET: Out of everything, that is probably the area in which it has so much value—resolving con-flicts. I have one technique in this area that I use here, and I call it "cage fighting."

GB: Can you explain?

JANET: Cage fighting occurs when you have con-flict going on, and you get all the people involved in that conflict—and often it's just two people—in the same room. You sit down and you address the conflict openly, but with respect and a moderator. I'm usually the moderator. It's getting those peo-ple together in that room and first identifying their strengths, what they are really good at, and making the other person recognize that. I'll ask, "What do you like about this person as a co-worker or a per-son?" And then we address the conflict in an adult way, taking ownership for your part in the conflict, and then determining what we're going to do going forward and holding each other accountable. I intentionally gave it a funny term, and it tends to make them smile. I think it lightens the mood.

Cage fighting is not for every situation. If we have a bad seed in the organization and they need to be managed out and they have no redeeming qualities, then they do not end up in a cage fight. Cage fighting is for good people, wonderful people who just need to resolve a conflict. So we get in a room, shut the door, and talk about it until it's worked out.

GB: Do you believe that Servant Leadership can be taught?

JANET: Yes. And I wish I could have taken a class in Servant Leadership. You know, I have an MBA and an undergraduate degree in Business, and I was never taught any of this. I think of the agony that it would have saved me had I been taught or been exposed to this material. It would have made me better and more confident sooner. I would have made fewer mistakes, and I would have been happier as a person. There would have been less stress in my life had I been exposed to that material early on. You know, people absorb their environment. Universities wouldn't exist, and we wouldn't believe in higher education, if we didn't think that it had an effect and an impact on people. There are some people who are never going to get it and are never going to be Servant Leaders. They are going to fail in business, no matter what. And then there are some people who are born to be Servant Leaders. So when I say that I think it can be taught, I think of the 20-60-20 rule. Twenty percent of the people will never get it, twenty percent of the people were born to get it, and the remaining sixty percent of people can be taught or influenced if they are exposed to material like this.

GB: Do you have role models who you admire and trying to emulate in your life?

JANET: One of the things that has given me comfort and been an example for me is just living in La Crosse, Wisconsin, and having what I think is a pretty strong base of family businesses. The people here are involved, charitable, intelligent leaders who are operating family businesses. To me that has been influential and positive. We have many examples in this community of successful family businesses that give back to the community. I think we are a very involved, close-knit, supportive community. We have good colleges, we have good healthcare, we have good social services, and a lot of these things are from very charitable people that run very good organizations that people want to work at. No one of us is perfect, but we can take something from each other and learn.

GB: The attitude of giving back is a characteristic of Servant Leadership, and, fortunately, we live in a community where many people understand that. Janet, if you could teach young people one thing, what would it be?

JANET: That today counts. Today counts! I see young people who seem to say, "This is what I'm doing right now, but someday I'm going to do X, Y, or Z." They have aspirations of what they are going to do "someday" and they don't realize that they are doing it today. It doesn't matter if they are digging a ditch or whatever. Today they are becoming who they will be. If they give themselves a hall pass not to care today, and not to care about other people, and not to do the right thing today, they can't magically turn it on someday. You can't magically become a wonderful person and a good leader by your watch. You have to practice it today. You have to do it today.

I hate to see young people who are not invested in their job today, don't come to work on time, don't work hard, because this is not the job they want to do. This isn't the career they have chosen.

Consequently, they never get to where they want to be because they aren't doing it today. You never know which person you meet or which impression you make that will become major in the future. So if you're not engaged in today, you'll never know how, but you're cutting off your future.

Reflections

The theme and focus of this interview centered on humility. I was speaking to someone who recognized and acknowledged the gravity associated with taking over the responsibilities of a family business. Couched in her humility of being asked to carry on the family business is the fact that Janet recognizes that being put in this position was a gift. While she and her sister purchased the business from their parents, she believes there should be a strong sense of dedication and responsibility that goes with someone who takes over the family business.

In the beginning, Janet was not sure that she had the personality make-up to run a long-standing, successful business. It wasn't until she realized that she possessed many Servant Leadership characteristics and that a successful leader can demonstrate those characteristics that she began to feel more comfortable in her inherited role. I think Janet is proof that you can be humble and still be recognized as a leader.

She does not take for granted that she inherited her position in this business because of her last name. I sensed that she sees herself as a steward of her family name and business.

Dealing with conflict is something that few people enjoy, and, having interviewed Janet, I think it is even more difficult for humble people who, according to her, are not always endowed with a lot of self-confidence. Her philosophy of taking some of the edge off of employee tension by calling her conflict-resolution strategy "cage fighting" is very creative. As she explains, the idea is that the best way to resolve conflict is for individuals to have the opportunity to express their feelings. Ideally, the outcome encourages compromising and forgiving. I know it is not that simple, and Janet didn't say that it was, but I do think "cage fighting" is a positive Servant Leadership practice to resolve conflicts. The reality is that conflicts happen, and unresolved conflicts can have a downward-spiraling effect. So it is important to have established practices in place when the need arises.

There was no hesitation when asked about her mentors. Her mom and dad both provided positive role models for her, and she was also quick to point out that she benefitted from observing unique characteristics and values from both.

To Think About

• How do you think about and process monetary and non-monetary gifts of significance which you have received?

• Do you have a pre-determined strategy for resolving conflicts?

• Do you feel comfortable in the positions you hold?

KRISTINA (SMABY) SCHOH

Kristina (Smaby) Schoh is a native of Holmen, Wisconsin, and a 2010 graduate of Viterbo University with a Bachelor's degree in Business Management. She currently works as the Community Relations manager for Courtesy Corporation, which owns and operates forty-four McDonald's restaurants in the Midwest. Her lifelong goal involves opening a national chain of intergenerational family support centers to provide integrated care for young and old alike. This passion stems from her longtime platform of "Connecting Generations." Kristina nurtured this idea in the La Crosse community while attending college. She hosted three Intergenerational Fairs in Holmen and La Crosse, and later organized two Intergenerational Proms at Viterbo University's Mathy Boys and Girls Club, where university students, nursing home residents, and the entire faith community, ages one to one-hundred, were welcome.

With her passion for community involvement, she reached her childhood goal of winning and reigning as Miss Wisconsin in 2009. Through competition in the Miss Wisconsin Scholarship Program, and the Miss America Pageant in 2010, she earned enough scholarship money to graduate debt-free . Today she shares her personal story while speaking to youth and community organizations. Kristina believes any success in her life comes from a strong faith and the ever-present will to persevere.

Let's Meet Kristina (Smaby) Schoh

GB: Kristina, what is your understanding of Servant Leadership?

KRISTINA: This concept has become familiar to me since my time at Viterbo University. When I first was introduced to it, and through conversations with people in the community and on campus with professors and other students, it just became evident to me that it's about being a natural leader and the natural feeling of wanting to serve others. It's not something that you can just say, "I'm a servant leader." You can't just give yourself that title. But you can say, "I was born to serve" or "I have a passion to serve" or "I love to serve others because it makes a difference."

GB: The other people that I interviewed for this book are at a stage in their lives or careers where they have risen to the top over the years. Because you are just starting out in your career, how do you think you will use Servant Leadership principles to move forward in your career?

KRISTINA: For myself, I have already chosen Servant Leadership as my foundation and plan to build on it. In the choices that I make, my reactions to different situations, whether in the workplace or at home, it's really the driving force as far as where I continue to go. I am twenty-five years old, and I feel I have already had the opportunity to serve others. But I know there are so many other opportunities ahead of me. Serving others isn't just volunteering or community service. It's the way you live your life. You can serve others in a meeting by listening, taking the time to care about what they're saying, and responding respectfully. The aspect of serving is night and day, not just at home or in the community or in the workplace.

GB: I suspect that you don't think someone is promoted or rises up the ladder by chance. Do you believe that, if you have the goal of using Servant Leadership principles, it will help propel you toward success?

KRISTINA: Sure. I think your bosses, your co-workers respect you if you treat them with respect. I've been here at Courtesy Corp. for about a year and a half, and so many of the employees have been here much longer, some over thirty years. So coming in here new, I needed to gain the respect of those who have been here and have put their time in, and I think one of the ways to connect with them is to serve them.

GB: It sounds as though you were using Servant Leadership principles even before you had a full understanding of what it meant.

KRISTINA: I learned to serve as a very young child. I thought of myself more as a leader, maybe a born leader. I like to create things that help people. That's always been something inside of me. But to really understand how to serve, you have to serve with dignity and respect. Those are two strong qualities that need to be in our workplace, that need to be in our homes, and hopefully that's how we create a positive culture. Everyone can be a Servant Leader. Everyone can have those strong qualities. It's just a question of having the confidence and the desire to do that, to be that kind of person.

GB: How do you think being a Servant Leader and demonstrating Servant Leadership characteristics have benefited you and the people you work with?

KRISTINA: It's created awareness for me. Not that I have changed extremely as a person, but I think that I have changed when it comes to my surroundings and my reactions to things that happen in my life. It's really helped me be more aware of the things I choose to say or the way I choose to listen when other people speak.

GB: Do you think your attitude about Servant Leadership helped you in being chosen as Miss Wisconsin?

KRISTINA: I think, ultimately, the judges do look for someone who is selfless, who is willing to put aside personal time to do something for others. You really have to be able to do that because you are giving up a year of your life. I gave up a year of my life with my family and my friends and my social time to travel to do things for the state of Wisconsin. It can't be all about you; it has to be all about others. At the same time, you have to give time and respect what you can do to nurture yourself and make sure that you are a healthy person, too.

GB: Do you think the judges saw that in you?

KRISTINA: It's tough to pinpoint that. I will say that one of the judges at the end of the competition came up to me and said, "Do you want to know what we all saw in you? You had great talent, you had fun on stage, you answered the questions well, you were well-spoken, and you interacted with the other contestants nicely. But the thing we saw in you was your inner light that showed through in every area of the competition." I took that to be more about my connection with my faith in God. That was what was amazing to me, that they saw not only the areas that I scored well in, but they also saw me for me and saw that deeper true meaning of that inner light.

GB: Do you think a successful person is a leader first and then becomes a Servant Leader, or are they a Servant Leader first who becomes a successful leader?

KRISTINA: I think it is a little bit of both. You definitely have to want to be a leader. You have to want to take the initiative, you have to want to be willing to help others. But serving—it's a natural feeling.

GB: Were you a leader in high school, too?

KRISTINA: Absolutely. I remember being a leader in elementary school. If there was a project to help someone, I was in. I remember collecting clothing for New Horizons, a domestic abuse shelter, in fifth grade. And when I won Miss Wisconsin, my fifth grade teacher sent me a picture of me hauling clothes out to the vehicle to take to New Horizons. That was a reminder to me. In fourth grade, I ran for class president, but I lost to the boy I had a crush on. I voted for him, and he won by one vote. That was my vote! I reflect back to those moments and realize I was a leader in elementary school.

A lot of that has to do with my mom. We started going to nursing homes when I was in elementary school because she always knew so many older folks that were in the nursing homes. She said, "Why don't you do this for them?" I think if parents raise children to serve, to lead, and to give back, then they are going to do that. They're going to carry that with them. I certainly give my mom a lot of credit for that. But your parents can only walk beside you for so long, and then it becomes your choice. It becomes your choice in high school, in college, and especially as a young professional in the work force. Luckily for me, I have had many experiences that have been positive and reminded me of the importance of serving people.

GB: Even though you are still young, I'm sure you have experienced conflicts in your life. Can you tell me how you have used Servant Leadership principles in resolving those conflicts?

KRISTINA: Even in the most minor of conflicts, just listening is so important. So often in conflict, we start to form our rebuttal in our minds as someone's giving their defense. Then they are thinking of what they want to say while I'm talking, and there is this ongoing mental battle. If we only took the time to listen, with no thought of what we want to say next. I think listening is the best way to resolve conflicts. That's something I feel I can do at work. I have a relationship in my family that I am trying to work on that more. It's an ongoing battle, and it has been a lifelong struggle for me, but that's one thing that I am really trying to work on. I think about the book *Left to Tell* by Immaculee Ilibagiza, where she epitomizes the act of forgiveness. Her story tells of her going up to the very person who killed her family and forgiving them. It's remarkable. If we all could have that attitude, it would be amazing. If we could all do that with just one person in our life, it would be life-changing.

GB: You've already covered this somewhat, but just to clarify, do you believe Servant Leadership principles can be learned, or taught?

KRISTINA: Certainly both. Again, you have to have an upbringing, an idea, an awareness of how to be a leader. You have to know how to give your time to others and not just yourself. Once you have that down, I think it can be taught, because this entire world of Servant Leadership was introduced to me as an eighteen-year-old. For some people, they may not learn it until they are thirty, forty, fifty, or even one-hundred.

GB: One of the purposes for writing this book is to make people aware of the principles of Servant Leadership in hopes that they will aspire to be Servant Leaders. Do you think that is possible?

KRISTINA: Absolutely. Viterbo University now offers a Master's degree in Servant Leadership. If I have a goal on my "bucket list," it would be to go back to school to do that. Some people might ask, "What will you do with that degree?" But it is a lifelong degree. It's something you are going to use until the day you die, because it is something to use with family, friends, people you meet at the grocery store. You learn how to smile at someone as you walk past, you learn how to care openly for people you may not even know. It's a remarkable gift. If it [the book] draws awareness, it's going to draw awareness in workplaces, in communities, in organizations, in our homes.

GB: You referred earlier to some of the influential role models in your life, and you mentioned Jesus and then St. Francis. When did you start recognizing that Jesus was demonstrating and lived the principles of Servant Leadership that guided you?

KRISTINA: I think there is the reminder every week when I'm sitting in church and looking up at the cross. I am reminded of that sacrifice, because serving is a sacrifice. I also think that just relying on different verses in the Bible that I turn to for struggles that I may be going through and seeing that almost every Bible verse references helping or serving, which is, ultimately, what a Servant Leader's foundation should be.

GB: If you could try to teach or show young people one thing, what would it be?

KRISTINA: Listen to everything. If someone is yelling at you, listen to them. If someone's sharing a story with you, listen to them. If you're outside walking in your neighborhood, listen to nature. If you're at work, take a half hour break and go somewhere and listen to what is going on around you. If you're not listening all the time, you're going to miss out on some of the most opportune moments that can be life-changing.

Reflections

My interview with Kristina was quite different than my other interviews. It was interesting to speak to someone who is at the beginning of her career. It was noteworthy to hear Kristina, at such a young age, express her clear understanding of Servant Leadership principles and characteristics. She is very much aware of the fact that, if you embrace those principles, it can help you achieve success in any given career.

Kristina gives proof that Servant Leadership characteristics can become parameters for your life at a very early age. She was very persistent in her pursuit of realizing her goal and dream of becoming Miss Wisconsin. Persistence is not considered one of the core Servant Leadership principles, but it can certainly be a positive attribute if you are helping and benefiting people along the way.

It was apparent that her faith in God serves as an anchor for her life. Turning to her faith when trying to overcome obstacles or struggles seems to have served her well.

She has learned, again at a very early stage, the

significance of employing the art of listening in her everyday life.

It would be interesting to do a follow up interview with Kristina twenty-five years from now to see where her ability to implement Servant Leadership in her career has taken her.

While I did not ask her to specify what her long-range goals are, I am sure she has them. Again, goal-setting is not typically described as a Servant Leadership principle; however, I do believe that the combination of practicing Servant Leadership principles and setting goals for yourself can positively lead to success.

I suspect Kristina will provide proof for that theory.

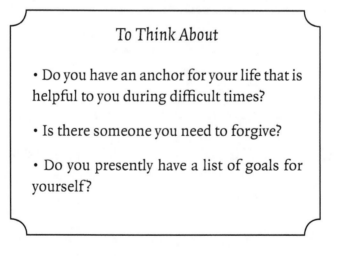

To Think About

• Do you have an anchor for your life that is helpful to you during difficult times?

• Is there someone you need to forgive?

• Do you presently have a list of goals for yourself?

Servant Leadership
in HEALTHCARE

What Is a Successful Leader in Healthcare?

If you have ever been cured of a serious illness, re-covered from a terrible accident, or broken bones, you would most likely judge the person or persons who provided care for you as successful. However, the people who provided that care may not necessar-ily be Servant Leaders. "My nurse or doctor had great bedside manners," is a quote we often say or hear about someone that dealt with us in a compassion-ate, attentive, respectful way.

A successful Servant Leader in healthcare helps to provide an atmosphere in their medical surround-ings of caring and going above and beyond the call of duty. They provide their patients with an air of confi-dence (that they are going to take good care of them) and compassion in dealing with the emotions of be-ing sick or broken.

Encouraging, giving, or creating camaraderie amongst co-workers can be positively sensed by the recipients of their care.

Accurate diagnostics, successful treatments, and positive outcomes of surgical procedures are incredibly important ingredients of healthcare providers. But the ability to demonstrate that a healthcare worker is concerned about you as an individual, and being able to reduce your stress and that of family members when you are dealing with illness or injury, is significantly important. I believe that the reduction of stress and the communication of confidence in the prescribed treatment can successfully affect a patient's outcome.

Achieving successful medical results is important but does not necessarily mean you are a successful Servant Leader in healthcare.

Being successful as an administrator in healthcare means you have the ability to lead in such a way that your colleagues catch your vision. They are inspired to provide the very best healthcare to their patients. Creating a positive atmosphere within the walls of the medical facility and between all healthcare staff assures patients that they are getting the best medical care available.

I tend to believe that the majority of healthcare providers are successful Servant Leaders. I am excited about sharing the thoughts and insights from two successful Servant Leaders in healthcare.

DR. JEFF THOMPSON

Our first stop is the office of Dr. Jeff Thompson, CEO and Chairman of the Board of Gundersen Lutheran Health Systems. Gundersen Lutheran is a multi-specialty group medical practice comprised of nearly seven-hundred medical, dental, and associate staff, and supported by a staff of more than six-thousand. It provides health services to patients at its hospital and clinics throughout western Wisconsin and north-central Iowa.

Although he serves as primary administrator for Gundersen Lutheran, Jeff still practices pediatric medicine and neonatology. He is also Chairman of the Board of the La Crosse Medical Health Science Consortium. Since completing his professional training in 1984, he has worked solely at Gundersen Clinic and Lutheran Hospital, and he played a key role in the negotiations and governance design that led up to the merger between those two healthcare entities.

Gundersen Lutheran has grown over the years to represent what healthcare should and can be. It consistently ranks among the top hospitals in the country, expanding its medical residency programs, its ongoing research protocols, and developing proactive community and global initiatives. Jeff has encouraged the development of Gundersen Lutheran's Global Partners program which reaches out to areas in Africa, the US, and Central America that are home to some of the poorest people in the world.

Dr. Thompson has authored a number of articles, book chapters, and abstracts on many healthcare topics, and, most recently, has been interviewed on both Wisconsin Public Television and National Public Radio concerning healthcare reform, using Gundersen Lutheran as the model of what healthcare should become in the future.

Let's Meet Dr. Jeff Thompson

GB: Jeff, let's start with a pretty basic question. What is your understanding of Servant Leadership?

JEFF: I have not taken a course or studied it, but I've certainly read a number of articles on it. My understanding is that there are probably a number of ways people are defining it academically. But in practice, I think of it as a description of a set of characteristics that address a combination of "values and practices" that develop a leadership style focused less on the leader and more on those the leader is responsible for. I choose the words "responsible for," because I use them all the time. You see a lot of things written about the requirement of a successful leader to hold people accountable. You have to hold people accountable. I think when you look at an organization, you build a much healthier organization and accomplish the same things if you look the other direction and say, "Who am I responsible for?"

I've got a slide I put up of our board chart where the patients are at the top, the clinical staff is responsible for the patients, and the managers and directors are responsible for the clinical frontline staff. The vice-presidents are responsible for the well-being and success of all the managers. And I'm responsible for all of those people. And, of course, the Board's responsible for me. They didn't particularly like it when I had them on the bottom of the pyramid, but they understood eventually. I think if you characterize it as being responsible, that is more consistent with the principles that you often see written about Servant Leadership, which is one of saying, "I have to hold them accountable to get these things done."

GB: Have you or do you think of yourself as a Servant Leader?

JEFF: I think it is very consistent with many of the ways I've tried to accomplish things. I think I could pick apart many of the decisions I've made or things I've tried to do that may not have hit the principles perfectly on the head, but I think the outcome of one's leadership is probably the best evaluation rather than my evaluation. So I would say you need to look to the people I work with.

If you can surround yourself with people who believe in something bigger than themselves and put their shoulders into it, and you have multiple people willing to do that, then you really can get some momentum. Then they attract people of similar values

Here's an example. We just came through a big economic downturn. The most common way for a big corporation, in the face of that, to balance their budget, certainly in healthcare, is to lay off large groups of people. I sat with my senior leadership group around the table and that topic came up, and my point to them was, if we have to lay off people to preserve the organizations, I understand that. But an organization our size, with our capability, if we get to that point it's because we at this table did not make good choices. So if we start layoffs, we start here. We will stay together. But here's what we're going to do. We're going to change this, we're going to change that, we're going to hold off on raises—we're going to try to preserve that. We slowed down on hires; we tried to double up on tasks.

Did we work extra hard and did we try to cut back on lots and lots of things? Yes. Did we have a mass layoff or delete Behavioral Health from our organization, as many did? We did not. Did we eliminate our education programs? We did not. Did we abandon things like our environmental program, or global health, or those things that are very consistent with our values? We did not do that. We said if it's about the patients and the staff, then it has to be about them all the time. And not just when things are going good and you're at the pinnacle and everybody's happy. It has to be about the hard times, as well.

So I think if you're going to lead with a focus broader than yourself, it starts with a value-set that is more translatable than the leader's responsibility. You can label yourself important and get awards and do positive things, but I think what really matters is who you are when you walk down the halls and talk to your peers. Do we have our own measurements that we look at? Yes, we measure like crazy. But we measure for the endpoint of serving the patients. Do I measure the vice-presidents and the directors? Yes, but I measure so they can serve their staff. So we measure hard, but it's the goal that's most important. It's the well-being of the patient, the well-being of the staff. Allowing them to take great care of the patients is a tremendous reward.

GB: Do you think a successful person becomes a leader first and then develops an attitude of serving others, or vice versa?

JEFF: I think it can happen either way, but I think it's probably easier vice versa. That is, I think it is easier for someone who believes in the well-being of others to rise up and lead than it is for a leader who is self-centered and self-important to see the light and change direction. I know it's happened, but I just believe it is easier the other way. I think a lot of people have an opportunity to lead in a very value-centered, servant-centered way. I think it grows up together in them.

When I look back on my lifetime, there are times when I've led, and there've been times when I bowed. There are times when I've felt badly about how self-focused I was. Trying to get A's all through college so I could get into medical school, studying like a crazy man my first two years in medical school to learn everything I could. We don't have a lot of time to breathe, let alone give back the way you'd like to and accomplish other things. These are periods you go through. This is certainly not based on any scientific study, but people I've seen who came from a strong religious or social heritage tended to lead at an early age and really seem to be well-grounded in their middle years.

I think of my college professor who was a bio-chemistry teacher and had a Mennonite background. I got to know him quite well when I was in college. Something came up about his love for gardening. He showed me his garden, and I said, "You've got five people in your family. You've got enough there for thirty people." He said he gardened to give it away. He had this massive garden, and he spent all fall harvesting it and giving it away. And he approached education that way. You had a responsibility to work, but if you met him half way, you got a tremendous education. He was terrific—a wonderful leader of faculty and his church and his community. It was not always about him. He rose up to be the number two guy in the university, sure to be the next dean. I recently got a note from him, and he has now stepped back from administration and he's back in the classroom.

I think we all have lots of opportunities to choose how we're going to behave in our leadership roles. The longer and the deeper it's been ingrained in us that others are more important than ourselves, and that we can do fine for ourselves without necessarily being on top of the heap, the more effective we can be.

GB: Who are the people who have had the most influence on you as a Servant Leader?

JEFF: I think early on, the clearest model would have been my mom. My mom—most people in society wouldn't consider her in the leader part of it, just the servant part of it. People think of me as outgoing, loud, and funny, but my mom was very quiet. My mom was the classic church secretary. She was the secretary of the Methodist Church, but she was the consummate servant. She took care of things; she took care of everybody. People who show up at the desk of a community church are pretty much the breadth of the population with a lot of different needs. She solved a lot of people's needs. It wasn't exactly part of her job description, but she did it. Pastors would come and go, and she kind of held everything together. Of course, this is her son's evaluation of the whole situation, but when she retired, it was a much bigger retirement party than any pastor who came and went. She was always behind the scenes, and led by example. So she had a very important influence on me.

We were raised in the Christian tradition of the Methodist Church which is less hierarchal, more scholarly and pretty focused on the typical person rather than the hierarchy of the church. I think that was a pretty significant thing.

Probably the third, in my younger years, would have been the people involved in Boy Scouts. We had some tremendous examples of tireless servants, principals of schools, superintendents of high schools, managers of big car dealerships, all of whom did lots of things. There was no reason they had to do this. We had a veterinarian who was a native Winnebago, now Ho-Chunk—such a hard worker, so thoughtful and so non-combative, non-confrontational. So my early years were pretty much shaped by my mom, Scouts, and this Christian background.

My middle years—it was a college professor and another person in medical school—she was Jewish— who had an East Coast Boston and New York edge to her. But she was an amazing server of the patients and the staff. She was all about saying, "We have a responsibility here. We volunteered to come to medical school. We volunteered to be this doctor in this residency program. Now take care of these patients as if they were your own. Take care of these people." She was all about the patients. It wasn't about fame or glory or anything about her. It was all about taking care of someone else. She was a wonderful, brilliant teacher, a noble human being. And when you got through the academic "futzing around," there was a person that was not there for fame and glory, not for stardom and not for a fancy position. It was all about saying we have a responsibility, a responsibility to these patients. We have volunteered to stand here and do this job. So focus on them. It's not about you; it's about them.

So you start adding up all those different influences, and I think you end up with a growing focus on saying there'll be plenty of opportunities to feel good about yourself. The best things about feeling good have to do with the accomplishments of those people for whom you're responsible.

GB: Jeff, do you think that those people—your mother, your teacher, Boy Scout leader—had any awareness that they were being a role model for you?

JEFF: Oh, I'm sure that my mom didn't. She just thought she's a mom and her job was to take care of me and worry that I didn't turn into a hood or the '60s version of a gangster. She worried about that. I got straight A's in high school, I played sports every season, I sang, I wrote, I was an Eagle Scout, but she still worried about me, so I don't think she ever thought that way.

I imagine the other leaders had some inkling of that kind of activity because, with most of them, it grew from an acquaintance to a really genuine friendship. So we connected at a deeper level. My guess is they would have. When I got older, I circled back to them and told them. I made a special effort to do that. I just felt it was important that they understood what an influence they had. They taught me that you can be a very successful leader, even in current tight environments, and not to focus on yourself but to focus on the well-being of the staff that you're responsible for and the people that you and your staff serve.

GB: You can't be in a position in a large organization like this without being confronted by some conflicts. How do you feel that you have used Servant Leadership characteristics and principles in trying to resolve conflicts?

JEFF: I think when you have a really strong set of values it allows you a baseline to do that. Now I used the example of the layoffs earlier, saying that we won't say "never," but we would say let's try everything else first, because it's really hard on people to lose their jobs in the face of a recession. We wouldn't take it off the table if it meant saving the organization, but short of that, let's try to do everything else first.

Let's say you are a medical staff member and you start doing your surgeries. Of your most common surgeries, four of them are going well and one of them is going poorly, and you've had some not-so-good outcomes. So you sit down and say, "Let's talk about this. Why do you think that is?" It just didn't happen. We have an obligation to our patients, and we have pretty high standards. So what we need is to have those outcomes improve. So we offer some options. "Let's have you scrub with this other more experienced surgeon." Or maybe the world's greatest surgeon doing this procedure is in San Diego, and we say, "You go there—we'll pay you to go there for two weeks and work with him and pick up a few things." Or something else that you might suggest. All those options are great. What is not acceptable— what we cannot have—is for nothing to change and the outcomes to stay the same.

So I think that's an approach to interpersonal development you can take. The first move is not to say it's okay, but to say, "What can we do to make them as successful as possible?" So we have education options for doctors, for nurses, for administrative personnel, for pharmacists—all these education things that we feel are part of our responsibility. Your responsibility is to get out of your chair and go take advantage of it. On the other hand, the baseline value is not how much money you are going to put on my books, or growing our egos—those are not the guiding principles. The guiding principle is the well-being of the patients or the frontline staff. So if your behavior hurts the frontline staff or your outcomes hurt the patient, that has to change. It actually makes it easy because here are these principles and you have a choice. You can live within them or not, and if you say not, then we'll find another place for you to work.

We were functioning that way, but then we codified it into a document called "The Physician's Compact." We had it for the leadership team, and now we have it for the staff, as well. It says "Here's what we're responsible for as an organization. We'll pay you fairly and provide a good environment. You'll be treated with respect. We'll give you good communication. You'll have an opportunity to learn and serve. Here's what you're responsible for. You'll treat everybody with respect. You'll work hard to communicate. You will champion quality and improvement." You give that to people as soon as they apply for a job and say, "If this doesn't sound like something you want to be a part of, then there's no point in continuing this interview, because this is how we operate." We believe that it is important to be consistent, and having a set of values and principles consistent with the Servant Leadership model makes it all easier. It makes it easier to hire, and it makes it easier to evaluate people who are going to function at high standards. They don't mind high standards, and, as it turns out, they're fine with it. We have very high quality standards.

My contention is that these baseline values—a set of principles that are consistent with Servant Leadership—can permeate a broader part of the organization and result in a service to the community. I sleep better at night knowing we are delivering on our promises to our patients.

GB: Why have you chosen to have a very simple office for yourself? I'm sure in most large hospitals, the CEO has a different type office than this.

JEFF: One of the things I did when I took over was that I changed the name of the leadership group. They were called the Executive Leadership group, and I changed it to Administrative Services. I told them our job is to serve. I remember when I was a medical vice-president and the hospital and the clinic came together, all of the offices were not that fancy. All of the vice-presidents took it as an opportunity to go out and buy thousands and thousands of dollars of cherry and mahogany furniture. People joked and called it Mahogany Row. I remembered that, and I also remembered what our main job is here—to take care of our staff and serve patients.

One of the reasons I went to an open floor plan here is that I wanted it clear to the staff and anybody that came in that our job was to take care of them, and we're all on the same team.

We were over on the second floor and it was pretty clear that the surgery area needed a place for families to stay. So I said, "That's it, we're out of here, and we're moving. Because the patients and families need this space, we don't." Some of the people lobbied to build a place offsite where we could have our own spot, be more efficient. I said, "No way. we're staying on the campus. We have to be close." My plan was to make it clear that we were humble and not arrogant, that we were there to take care of the staff and not hide from them. We are there to take care of each other, and we have an open environment. Anybody's problem is everybody's problem.

GB: What is your idea about Servant Leadership principles being either taught or learned?

JEFF: I absolutely think it can be taught and learned. There are basic principles that can be outlined, and there are real-life examples that can be brought in, so that it's a mix of the academic side of it and the real-life experience side of it. And I think these kinds of things absolutely can be learned. I believe it not only is possible, but it would be very valuable for organizations to formalize their approach to Servant Leadership principles more. Just like our "Compact." We made it really clear what our expectations were and that tends to attract people. It makes it perfectly clear what the expectations are, but also to have the part that says, "Here's where we are headed, here's what we're looking for, here are the ideals that we're going to work for. We are going to help you learn, we're going to help you train, we're going to have an environment around you that supports these kinds of principles." And then the organization has to deliver.

GB: What would be the most important value that you would like to pass on to our young people of today?

JEFF: I would encourage young people to maximize their potential in all areas of their life and to use all of the gifts they have been blessed with. I would want them to know that your values are second to courage, because you have to have the courage to live up to your values

Reflections

When I left Jeff Thompson's office, I felt very secure and comfortable in knowing that the Gundersen Lutheran Clinics and Hospital were in good hands.

Jeff's whole focus in his professional career is seeing that the people who come to GLC for their healthcare needs receive the very best service available. His entire emphasis is on service, and the most important people on his staff are the people that are directly providing those services to the end user, the patient. He puts a great deal of emphasis on the fact that everyone that is a part of GLC is a part of a team. He not only demonstrates this by his words and actions, but also through his humble office environment. This in and of itself implies that he does not see himself as being more important than anyone else on the team. The emphasis he puts on building team support and collaboration is certainly a characteristic of Servant Leadership.

While Jeff realizes and understands the fact that a team needs a leader, he also realizes the significance of everyone buying into the team leader's vision. How you get people to buy into that vision is a major objective for him.

Enjoying what a Servant Leader does was very evident in listening to his answers and to his enthusiasm. He appears to be a man of strong conviction and uses the principle of leading by example. Making the many service teams at GLC aware of Servant Leadership principles and how those principles can enhance service to patients is encouraged from the top.

Several times Jeff mentioned his Methodist upbringing, and I was curious about the basic tenets of that religion. It can easily be summed up in the words of its founder John Wesley:

> Do all the good you can,
> By all the means you can,
> In all the ways you can,
> In all the places you can,
> At all the times you can,
> To all the people you can,
> For as long as you can.

It would seem that John Wesley understood Servant Leadership, and Jeff lives his life by that philosophy.

To Think About

• Are you leading others in a positive way through your examples?

• Do you consider yourself as an equal to your peers?

AMANDA BUCKLES

My next visit took me back in the presence of someone I had come to know quite well this past year. Amanda Buckles came into my life at a very difficult time. She was a registered nurse on the Intensive Care Unit at Gunderson Lutheran Hospital where my son was a comatose patient for more than two months. In my frequent visits to Jason's bedside, I often saw Amanda, and over time got to know her and the many wonderful supportive nurses and staff caring for our son. Amanda was special, always greeting me with a hug, lots of empathy, and boundless compassion. I watched the way she treated Jason's motionless body, always treating him with the utmost respect and enormous patience. She treated all of Jason's family—his parents, his wife and four daughters, his sisters—in the same way. It made all us more comfortable knowing that he was under such compassionate care.

You could tell immediately that Amanda was a person who cared about the well-being of others. She was the kind of person with whom we felt comfortable sharing and expressing the many emotions we were all experiencing. She is presently pursuing classes at Viterbo University in an effort to advance her education in nursing.

Let's Meet Amanda Buckles

GB: The reason I wanted to interview you is that you came into our lives at a really difficult time. You seem to have a great ability to show your concern and compassion. I want to begin our interview by asking you to share your understanding of Servant Leadership.

AMANDA: When I think of a Servant Leader, I think of someone who is genuinely good and actively doing good unto others. It's a concept I think we all essentially understand, but I never heard it called "Servant Leadership" until recently.

GB: It is a fairly new concept. Do you think of yourself as a Servant Leader?

AMANDA: I just don't know that I deserve to be labeled as a Servant Leader. When I think of a Servant Leader, I think of someone who has done a lot of great things in their life, and I don't think that I have. I can appreciate that I'm a compassionate person, and I do love my job.

My connection with you and your family was so valuable to me. I think of your family all the time, and I feel like I have that with my patients a lot; but I just never thought of myself as a Servant Leader.

GB: I assure you, Amanda, in my opinion riches and fame do not necessarily define a Servant Leader. You are just as much a Servant Leader as other people I mentioned to you. That's why I wanted to interview you, because I really hope that I can convince people that you don't necessarily measure a person's personality or the way they treat people by the fame that they have claimed or the riches they have gained. Do you want to be recognized as a Servant Leader?

AMANDA: Of course I do. I think that everyone wants, in one way or another, to have those qualities, doing what they can for the greater good. Just doing well for others and those around them. And I have to agree, I don't think success is measured by fame or wealth, but some of the people you mentioned—I don't know them, but I imagine they have done a lot more than I have.

GB: Success is measured in many different ways, and again, that is one of the reasons I chose you to interview. Do you think a successful person becomes a leader first and then develops an attitude of serving others, or is it vice versa?

AMANDA: I think it almost has to be in them before they get to the point where they are considered by others as a Servant Leader. I think it's part of their nature first, and everything develops after that. By having those qualities and being a Servant Leader, I think you become a leader and then become successful.

GB: Who are the people who have had the most influence on the person you are today?

AMANDA: My grandmother. My parents, of course, and my immediate family, but my grandparents were a very big part of my growing up. My grandma and I had a very special bond from the time that I was a very small girl. When she was sick, I was with her a lot, and that's when I decided to become a nurse. I think by nature I've always been a "motherly" person, nurturing, but I knew then that I wanted to put it in my career. She was just such a positive influence in my life; she was just so selfless.

GB: What did you admire about her the most?

AMANDA: She was just so giving, such a strong woman, but she was silent about it. She didn't need any recognition. She was such a good person, and she didn't need anyone to know that. She gave everything that she had for everyone else and she didn't need very much in return. I spent a lot of time with her as a child and even into my adult years. My daughter and I would go back and stay with them a week at a time. I think she's a part of who I am today. My parents are a big part of who I am today, as well, but I just had a really special bond with my grandma. Anyone who knew us would tell you that.

GB: Is there someone you have used as a role model that you have looked up to, respect, and even would like to pattern your life after?

AMANDA: I have several. I have a number of wonderful friends who are strong women and strong characters, and they have really been a big support for me in everything I have gone through in my life. That would be in my personal life. I have a big group of strong women around me that I know are always going to be there for me. In my wedding, I had ten bridesmaids, because I have such wonderful friends, and I couldn't pick between them. I am so lucky that way. They are all such beautiful people. I've always had them as a support group, and I look up to all of them.

And then on a professional level, as nurses we always have to be aware of how we can be better and how we can take better care of our patients. In my unit, the unit that I work on, we have such a group of strong women—and men, too. We have a very big team effort there, and without that we wouldn't be able to do our jobs every day. There are several people that I look up to very much.

I would have a hard time selecting just one person as a role model. I have a lot of people in my life who have a lot of good qualities, and they have supported me and have made me a better person. I know I have an idea of the kind of person I want to be, and although there is not one particular person that I can say is my mentor or my role model, I can say that I fully appreciate the good qualities in all of the people I am close with and work with.

GB: Do you think that Servant Leadership and being a nurse go hand in hand?

AMANDA: Yes, I do.

GB: What percent of nurses do you think portray the characteristics of Servant Leadership?

AMANDA: I think all of them have some of the Servant Leadership characteristics, but I think it is really hard for someone to possess all the characteristics that I think you would want to see in a Servant Leader. I think every nurse has to have honesty, integrity, and compassion. You can't be a good nurse without some of those qualities.

GB: Have you ever seen people that are in nursing that discovered they didn't have those characteristics and discovered that nursing was not for them?

AMANDA: I think I've met someone that was beyond that point in their life. I don't think I've ever worked with someone who was practicing as a nurse and still knows that about themselves. In fact, I think as soon as someone knows that about themselves, they would move on. And the great thing about nursing is that there are career paths you can take that are not patient-care driven—not direct care—and I think those individuals have taken themselves into more of an administrative role. I don't know how to say that without making it sound like people who don't care about people go into administration. That is not what I mean at all. I just think that they find another role that suits them better as a person, and I think that, overall, that's better for everyone.

GB: In your role as a nurse I'm sure you have had to deal with conflict. How do you think you have used Servant Leadership principles in trying to resolve those conflicts?

AMANDA: The thing that I always remember is that

this is someone else's experience, and it's probably one they've never gone through before. Being a patient in a hospital is a very vulnerable thing. You're at the mercy of those people who are taking care of you and the people that are in charge of your well-being for the most part. I think it's something that, as a nurse, I have to be aware of. If there is conflict or something that is making it difficult for there to be a good rapport, you have to keep in mind your compassion and your awareness that this person is an individual, and they need to express themselves the way they need to.

GB: Do you have any examples of experiences where you sensed there was a conflict between you and a patient, or you and a colleague?

AMANDA: Yes. Not often, but it's always hard to know how to handle them. There are so many personalities involved. Not only do you have a different personality for each nurse, but each patient is different, with different needs and different responses. We're an acute care setting, and that means you constantly have new people coming and going. It's hard under the best of circumstances to build a rapport in the twelve hours you spend with that person. Add in the stress of the situation, for both the patient and their loved ones, and it's even harder. You have to bury your own judgments because, ultimately, it's not about you.

GB: The basic qualities of Servant Leadership are being honest, considerate, concerned, being patient, trustworthy, and compassionate. I've seen you demonstrate all of those. How do you think those characteristics have benefited you? How has having those virtues had a positive impact on how you live your life?

AMANDA: I think it most definitely helps me do my job. On a professional level, it helps me build relationships with patients I have a short time with, and some patients longer, but I'm very grateful that I can open up and be a caring person. Not everyone can do that. As I said, I've always been a very caring and nurturing person, and I've always wanted to take care of other people. I think that just transcends from my personal life to my professional life, as well.

GB: Does it make you feel good about yourself to be able to demonstrate those characteristics?

AMANDA: Definitely. I'm grateful for being able to have a close relationship with my co-workers and, of course, my family, and it makes me feel very good that I can put people at ease. I know with your family, I felt a strong bond with you and I looked forward to your coming in, and that made me feel wonderful. Just the fact that I could offer a hug to make you feel a little bit better was important to me. I think one of the biggest things for me is knowing that when a family leaves, they know that they don't have to worry. They know I'll take good care of their mom or dad or whoever it might be, and that makes me feel good—really good.

GB: Do you believe that you are born with Servant Leadership principles, or that you learn them?

AMANDA: I think a little bit of both. The whole thing of "nature vs. nurture" debate has gone on for years. I think you are born who you are, but I also think it is something that can be taught. I think it may be something that's contagious. If you live your life day to day and you're a happy, positive person and you do good for others, it may trickle down or trickle across to other people. I think if you're surrounded by those Servant Leadership qualities, eventually you're going to catch some of them.

GB: That is one of the reasons I'm writing this book. Hopefully, sharing these thoughts with other people has the potential to make this a better place to live and a better place to work. So, finally, if you could teach young people, and give them one piece of advice, what would it be?

AMANDA: Always strive for what you want to achieve, and make sure, while you're doing that, that you are putting your best foot forward. Be yourself, and be who you want to be, but always remember that who you are is going to affect someone else. Always treat others as you would want to be treated. This may be a generational thing, but I feel a lot of our youth are just expecting things to come to them and feeling that they do not have to work for it. We're losing focus on trying to be a good person, and being accountable, and focusing on what's really important in life, because some of those things aren't always achievements or success.

GB: What would be your advice to those people who would read this book?

AMANDA: Search within yourself and find those good qualities, because I think everyone possesses at least a few of the qualities of a Servant Leader. So just find those and use them in what you do every day by being a good person, a positive person, trying to pass that on to others. Sometimes I think we lose sight of those types of qualities that we have because we're so busy being a mom or a dad or an employee.

GB: You are a mom. Do you see yourself demonstrating any of the characteristics of Servant Leadership in your role as a mom?

AMANDA: I hope so. I really hope so.

Reflections

It was refreshing to visit with Amanda and to reflect on the uniqueness that she brings to the concept of Servant Leadership. She realizes and appears to be comfortable with the fact that her virtues of Servant Leadership have not brought her fame or fortune. However, as I shared with her, fame and fortune are not always synonymous with Servant Leaders. More important than fame and fortune is the way people feel or respond to you as a human being.

Humility appears to be a virtuous characteristic that emanates from her personality. Humility does not denigrate the concept of a Servant Leader; instead, it can help identify and even magnify an individual as a Servant Leader.

There is much to be learned from Servant Leaders such as Amanda. I believe that a positive result of her kind of Servant Leadership is that she and many other Servant Leaders are very comfortable within their skin. To be comfortable with who you are, and what you do, should be an attitude that we all strive to possess.

As a recipient of Amanda's practice of Servant Leadership principles, I can attest that perhaps her strongest characteristic is the ability to empathize with her patients, their family and friends. There are many skills that Amanda uses in her practice and everyday duties as a nurse, but how those skills are played out and given can make a huge difference in a very stressful time in the lives of others.

On this journey, I thought it was very important to include an interview with someone like Amanda. Amanda's name is not as well-known as those of my other interviewees; however, being well known or having her name recognized in large circles of people is not important to her. As I said earlier, fame and fortune are not always congruent or desired. Rather, being a positive role model and practicing Servant Leadership principles in everyday life is what matters.

Our family will be forever grateful for the empathy and compassion that she shared with us.

To Think About

• Do people feel like they can talk to you?

• Do you show empathy in the way you communicate with others?

• Is this something you would like to improve upon?

Servant Leadership
in POLITICS

What Is a Successful Leader in Politics?

I thought about how to answer this question for a long time. Obviously, how many elections a politician wins and by what margins is a significant way to measure success in politics. Politicians are elected by constituents who subscribe to the platforms and promises that are made during the campaign. Some politicians are better at campaigning than others. Some are better than others at raising campaign funds. And, of course, the more money they raise, the more opportunities they have of getting their name and face in front of the public.

I sincerely believe that most people who desire to be elected as a public servant do so with the very best of intentions. They see problems or concerns in their community, their state, their country, and they honestly want to do something to make a difference. It is my opinion that those politicians who continue to vote their convictions are the most successful.

It must be very tempting for politicians to accept favors or money from individuals or groups who want them to vote for the causes they are promoting. Politicians who do not allow themselves to become obliged to special interest groups and are not tempted to change their vote because of that are, in the long run, the most successful. I suspect that is why they continue to get re-elected. I also suspect that most people, even if they don't agree with the politician's viewpoint, respect politicians who vote for what they believe in and what they feel is the best for their community, state, or country.

Politics has the capability of having people look at the very same set of circumstances and have totally opposite viewpoints. We all know about how political situations can be "spun" according to the desired outcome. The ability to be able to convince people that a certain view is the right one is what contributes to a politician's success. Practicing Servant Leadership principles in politics will often influence people when they cast their votes. When constituents feel that they are being listened to by their representatives, and that their concerns and questions are being addressed in a respectful manner, their votes will usually follow that candidate at election time. Success, in turn, is bound to follow. For a politician to hold strong and true to his or her convictions, even though it could cost them an election is, in my opinion, the sign of a successful leader.

GOV. TOMMY THOMSON

The next person I was directed to by my GPS screen is known to people all across the state of Wisconsin and, in recent years, the country.

From 1987 to 2001, Tommy Thompson served as the 42nd Governor of Wisconsin, having been elected to an unprecedented four terms.

Thompson's initiatives during his thirteen-year tenure included his Wisconsin Works welfare reform program and school choice program, which allowed low-income families to send children to the private or public school of their choice. He also created the Badger Care program designed to provide health-care coverage to those families without healthcare because their employers don't provide health insurance and they make too much money to qualify for Medicaid.

Through the federal waiver program, Thompson helped replicate this program in several states when he was appointed Secretary of Health and Human Services by President George W. Bush.

He began his career in public service in 1966 as a representative in Wisconsin's State Assembly. He was elected assistant Assembly minority leader in 1973 and Assembly majority leader in 1981. Thompson has received numerous awards for his public service, including the Anti-Defamation League's Distinguished Public Service Award. In 1997 he received *Governing Magazine*'s Public Official of the Year Award and, in 1998, the Horatio Alger award.

He has served as chairman of the National Governors' Association, the Education Commission of the States and the Midwestern Governors' Conference. He saw duty with the Wisconsin National Guard and the Army Reserve. At this time, Tommy sits on the boards of many corporations across the country and is a partner at the law firm of Akin Gump Strauss Hauer & Feld.

His resume certainly qualifies him to speak on the topic of Servant Leadership.

Let's Meet Gov. Tommy Thompson

GB: Tommy, you have had such an interesting career, and I am sure that you can credit your success to many things. I am wondering if you feel that your ability to practice the principles of Servant Leadership contributed to your success, and while answering that, would you please share your understanding of the concept of Servant Leadership?

TOMMY: I really don't understand what you mean by Servant Leadership. My impression of leadership is one of hard work, high ethics, and being an individual that people want to follow based upon your common sense, your intelligence, your hard work, and your ethics. You have to be able to command a leadership position, and you have to earn that. It cannot be given to you. The same people you compete with may be a lot smarter, a lot better-looking, and so on and so forth. But they can't accomplish the same thing because they don't have the drive, the ethics, the work ethics, or the honesty and the integrity that people believe in and want to follow.

I've always lived by certain rules. One is that you can't accomplish much if you don't really participate. You have to first be a participant in order to lead and win and succeed. Second, you have to do it by hard work. You can't expect other people to do it for you. You have to do it for yourself. If you work really hard, people will pitch in and help you. The third thing you have to do is be completely honest. I think it was Abraham Lincoln who said, "You can never outlive a lie." You always have to be honest. I think I was known for the fact that both sides of the aisle always knew that they could come to me and talk to me, and if I gave them my word, they could go back with it.

There was one incident that I'll always remember. It had to deal with not starting school until after

Labor Day. I lost friends over it, but I lived by my ethics. It was a position that I wanted to support, and, in fact, I put it in the budget bill. But then some legislators voted to take out the provision for not starting school until after Labor Day. And there was a compromise, and one of the legislators who's now a state senator came to me and said, "I don't like the provision." And he said, "I'm going to vote for this thing, but I don't believe in it, and you need to veto it." And I said, "Why do I have to veto it?" And he said, "Because I won't vote for it, and you won't get your budget bill. My position is I will vote for it, if you promise me that you will veto that provision." I said, "That's my provision." And he came back, "I'm telling you, I will not vote for your budget if that provision's in there, because you don't have enough votes to do it. So I will vote for that provision with the understanding between you and me that you have to veto it."

It was tough because all of Wisconsin Dells' business people had put it in and supported it, really believed in it. But later I vetoed it, because I gave the man my word that I would. Nobody knew about it, but I gave him my word, and that's how I live my life. I don't write things down like most people do. I'm a lawyer. I'm the one that should be writing things down. But I believe what my papa taught me. If you shake hands, look a person in his eye and you tell him something, you got to believe it. And that's how I live my life.

GB: What is your view on how some people have become successful but didn't practice Servant Leadership ethics?

TOMMY: They're on quicksand. If you don't have the underpinnings and you are able to camouflage and hide those principles and get ahead with sleight of hand, or through being dishonest, it may not happen immediately. But sooner or later, the dishonesty and the lack of ethics will catch up with you and will, eventually, bring you down. Those individuals who do that probably will not reach their full potential, because they have not cemented in their cornerstones correctly. They can still achieve a certain degree of success because they've shown the ability to defraud, confuse, or camouflage. It's an ability they have. But if they would use that ability for more meritorious things and build on that, they would have the potential to climb much higher. I look at those individuals and say they got ahead, probably not by doing the right things, but so and so could have done a heck of a lot more. If they had done it right, they probably could have achieved higher successes. But they are now probably being penalized in the world of public opinion.

GB: Do you think that a person becomes a leader first and then develops an attitude of serving others or vice versa?

TOMMY: I don't think you can become a leader without building upon the principles. You can ascribe to being a leader, but you have to build it. You have to learn to build upon that leadership. You have to do it in a way that is ethical and noble and be involved with serving people. My whole political life has been about how to give the best service to the maximum number of people. I'm not always going to agree with them, but even those individuals who don't agree with me have a right to be served by me, because I represent them. I have to listen to them and talk to them and communicate with them. I always had an open door policy, no matter who it was. There were people who wanted to come in and yell at me, and I said, "Come on in and yell." I always met with people. The Governor's office was always open. Many times, I would just open the office to anybody who wanted to come in and sit down and chat with the Governor. I loved it. But sometimes you get told some things you don't want to hear.

I did something that nobody's ever done before. One of the things I'm known for is that I changed welfare in America. Everybody knows that. But do you know how I got my ideas? I invited welfare mothers from different areas in Wisconsin to have lunch with me in the Governor's mansion. They never ever expected to meet a Governor, let alone have lunch with him. I would close the doors, and I wouldn't have any aides present. We sat around a big table and just chatted. I asked a welfare mother from Milwaukee why she didn't work. She said, "Why should I work? I get welfare and healthcare now if I don't work." So I said, "What if we got you healthcare? Would you work then?"

It took them a long time to warm up. I'd say, "My name is Tommy," and they'd say, "I can't call you Tommy," and I'd say, "Yes you can." And then somewhere along the line, one of them said, "Healthcare is great, but I have five kids. Who's going to take care of them if I go to work?" And I said, "What if we provided daycare for you?" And then someone said, "Yes, but I have no skills. I got pregnant when I was thirteen or fourteen, and my mother was on welfare, I'm on welfare. I have no skills." And I said, "What if we gave you training in the vocational school system? Would you work then?" And another one said, "Yes, but I live in the center of Milwaukee, and the jobs are out in the suburbs. How am I supposed to get there?" And I said, "What if we get busses or cars to transport you out there to work. Would you work then?" Then they finally started to say, "Oh, yeah!"

So I developed a program for welfare mothers. *The Milwaukee Journal* excoriated me for making people go to work. But the reason I was so successful with it was because those welfare mothers became so supportive. It was because I brought them in, talked with them, and had the courage to listen to them.

GB: Who are some of the people in your life that have made Tommy Thompson who you are today? Who are some of the key players in your life whom you feel that you have used as role models?

TOMMY: I had leaders all the way. The best leader I ever had was my father. He was a tough German, and he was very authoritarian to the extent that if a child had to live the way I lived, there would be hell to pay today. When I was six, I was cleaning eggs in the basement of the Thompson Grocery Store. If I wanted something, my father said, "You want something? You work for it." The farmers would bring eggs in, so he gave me the assignment of cleaning them. It was a dirty job. I hate eggs to this day. He had me paint barns. By the time I was twelve, I was up forty feet on a ladder painting barns. But he taught me that work is good. You don't accomplish anything without work. The second thing he taught me was that you don't steal and you don't lie. I stole some firecrackers once out of his store, and he caught me and he spanked me so hard that I never ever was tempted to steal again.

My mother was just the opposite. She was Irish, and she was just as gentle and sweet as could be. She once said to me, "Tommy, you've got two ears and one mouth. Use them in that proportion." My mother was a schoolteacher, and everybody loved her. Everybody was afraid of my father, but everybody loved my mother, the kindest and most generous lady I've ever had the privilege to know.

When I went to school, it was Mrs. Rogers and Mrs. Grange. I went to a little two-story school house. The first floor was Mrs. Grange and the second was Mrs. Rogers. They were a tremendous influence on me. They taught me how to study hard and get a good education.

In high school, it was Mr. Clare, who was an old football player from Platteville, and he imbued the love of geography and history in me. And he was also a great disciplinarian. He taught me you can't learn something if you don't listen.

And then I went to college, and I can remember certain professors who influenced me. I can remember a couple of my history professors, and my political science professor who was a large liberal Democrat. I had to write a paper, and he said, "You're a Republican, and you're too conservative, but I'll still give you an A."

And then in politics, there was the Speaker of the Assembly, and a federal judge who taught me how to be a leader. I always wanted to learn more. I always wanted to know the basic mechanics. I wanted to learn the rules of the legislature more than anything else, even though we were in the minority. I knew the rules backwards and forwards. I memorized them, and I could quote them on the floor.

And then I went to Washington. Vern Thompson was our Congressman and was my supervisor. I learned from him that hard work pays off. I was not overly impressed with his manner, even though he took me under his wing. I thought to myself, I can do this job better than he can. I learned that if you work hard, believe in your convictions, and you pursue them in a gentlemanly sort of way, you can accomplish many things.

GB: In situations where you wanted someone to like and respect you, and you felt like they didn't, what did you do? How did you deal with it?

TOMMY: I told them why I could or could not do something. You have to be honest. When you're the Governor, there's an emergency every day. Every single day, somewhere—and it's a good day when there's only one emergency—but there will be an emergency. Maybe it's small, maybe it's one that's going to require a lot of time, but you've got to deal with it. However, you cannot always have people like you. Somebody has elected you Governor to make decisions. You have to believe in what you're doing. You have to listen, but then you have to make the decision. Sometimes it's very lonely at the top, but if you believe that it's the right decision, then everything else falls into place.

GB: If you could teach young people today just one thing, what would you encourage them to learn or think about?

TOMMY: Never, never undersell yourself. Never underestimate your abilities. And always believe in yourself. Believe your inner self. Trust your gut. If your gut tells you that you can do something, you

163

can do it. And go after it. I'm a big gut believer. Every time I go with my gut, almost ninety-eight per cent of the time I'm right. If I go with my heart, I'm usually wrong. And above all, always be true to yourself. Be true to yourself because you're the only one the next morning that has to look at yourself in the mirror. If you can look at yourself in the mirror and say, "I did what I thought was right," even though it was not popular, you will get ahead faster and better and live a much more contented life

Reflections

The prominent thought that ran through my mind as I ended my interview with Tommy (he prefers to be called "Tommy") was how enthusiastic he is about what he is doing and what he has done. It's always my hope to leave each interview with one or two key thoughts that stand out in front of all the others. In this case, it was interesting to hear how much emphasis Tommy put on the core values of life that he learned from his mother and father. It appears that he did a good job of gleaning the best qualities from each. He can easily point to very specific experiences that taught him something and qualities from each that he tries to emulate in his own life.

Working hard does not appear to be a difficult task for Tommy. I suspect that he would become restless if he did not have a full agenda every day. I also think that he is happiest when he knows he is helping others. Even though Tommy confessed that he did not have a good understanding of the concept of "Servant Leadership," he certainly emulates its definition. "I was born to serve others," might be an appropriate title for a biography about this man. Tommy has already etched for himself a wonderful legacy that will succeed him for many decades to come. However, I think his biography is far from complete, because he is always going to keep himself busy, whether in politics, collaborating with different businesses across the country, or just serving others in some humanitarian way.

It was enjoyable to interview someone who has accomplished so many things that so few people have been able to do. And those accomplishments did not just happen. I believe they developed and succeeded because of his hard work ethic, compassionate communication, positive attitude in life, respect for others, willingness to listen to the viewpoints of others, and his never-ending desire to serve.

To Think About

• Do you work up to your potential?

• How well do you listen to the viewpoints of others?

• Are you enthusiastic about what you do?

SPEAKER DENNIS HASTERT

As a Congressman whose constituency came from the cornfields of Illinois, Dennis Hastert was honored by his colleagues when he was elected Speaker of the House of Representatives on January 6, 1999, the third highest position in the U.S. government. Serving until January 3, 2007, Hastert became the longest-serving Republican Speaker in history.

During his tenure as Speaker, Hastert focused his efforts on lowering taxes, improving education, strengthening Social Security and Medicare, and fortifying our national defense. In the response to the tragic attacks that occurred on September 11, 2001, he was instrumental in passing important anti-terrorism legislation to create a Department of Homeland Security.

Hastert drew from his experience as a former wrestling coach by emphasizing team-building and setting clear achievable goals. Colleagues recognized his ability to reach across the aisle in order to develop bipartisan legislation.

Hastert spent the first sixteen years of his career teaching government, history, and economics at Yorkville High School in Illinois. It was there that he met his wife, Jean, a fellow teacher. In addition to teaching, he coached football and wrestling, eventually leading Yorkville to victory at the 1976 Illinois State wrestling championship. Later that year, he was named Illinois Coach of the Year. Hastert, a former high school and college wrestler himself, was inducted as an outstanding American into the National Wrestling Hall of Fame in 2000.

Let's Meet Speaker Dennis Hastert

GB: Dennis, what is your understanding of Servant Leadership?

DENNIS: I taught for sixteen years in high school in the area of economics, government, and history, the substance of what you do in government. I was also a coach in football and wrestling. I think I learned early on, from those experiences, the value of being able to give back and to contribute on an ethical basis.

GB: How do you think your use of Servant Leadership principles helped you get to where you are today?

DENNIS: First of all, I never planned to be a member of Congress. It just kind of happened. I was teaching, and I saw a flier about running for the legislature in Illinois. So I decided to run and, surprisingly, I won. I served for six years in that capacity.

Then something strange happened. When things were shaping up for the next congressional campaign in the district in which I lived, three days after the primary, two of the Congressmen resigned their nominations because they both were informed they had terminal illnesses. So there I was, and I thought if I am ever going to run for Congress, now is my chance. So I did, and I won. I never dreamed it would happen.

I served for eight years in the minority, and then in 1994 our party took the majority, and I was named Chief Deputy Whip. I served in that position for four years while Newt Gingrich was Speaker. I did all the healthcare stuff, and a lot in the area of anti-drug legislation. At that time, we were losing sixteen-thousand kids a year to illegal drugs. If that many young people had died in a war, can you imagine the outrage? So I figured that was one of the biggest things I could do to try to make life better for people.

I also was the point man on Mrs. Clinton's [then the First Lady] healthcare task force in which it was decided that we would talk about philosophy and not policy. And then some of us wrote our own bill that essentially defeated her bill. Our bill let the free enterprise system take care of healthcare.

When Newt stepped down, I was ready to leave Congress. I thought I had a pretty good run—four years of being involved in all these areas. I didn't really think that I would fit in that well with the new leadership. So I figured I would do something else. I actually had an appointment with a head hunter. The day before that appointment, Bob Livingstone, who was expected to be the next Speaker, decided to step down, and suddenly people were turning to me and saying, "You're going to be the next Speaker." I said, "Why me, Lord?"

I ended up being Speaker for the next eight years. It's an incredible opportunity because you can do many things and have the opportunity to meet so many interesting people. Every piece of legislation, every government issue that happens, you are right in the middle of it. Then when 9/11 happened during my third year of Speakership, I went from a peace-time Speaker to a war-time Speaker. We had the responsibility to make sure that never happened to this country again. It was an interesting and challenging time.

GB: Since people were looking at you to be the next Speaker, and you weren't even running, they must have chosen you on the basis of some Servant Leadership characteristics you exhibited.

DENNIS: Leadership is based on trust, and if you don't have trust, you really cannot lead people. All those years that I was Chief Deputy Whip, I had to "whip" folks every day. People don't want to tell you how they're going to vote until they get onto the floor. But it is important to know how people are going to vote before you bring a piece of legislation to the floor. So the "Contract with America" and all the things we did after that—I was the guy who had to knock on their door and say, "How are you going to vote on this?" I had to call them at night. I knew where they hid out at night, when they hid out in the cloakroom when they wanted to get away from everything. As a part of my job there was a trust that built up over time. I could call them at home—I knew their wives, their kids. I never promised them anything, because you never knew if you could deliver on a promise or not because of various circumstances, but I would tell them what I could do and tell them if I could do more, I would. People always trusted what I said. My philosophy was to "under-promise and over-produce."

GB: So they trusted you because you were honest.

DENNIS: I think so.

GB: Trust and honesty are certainly important characteristics of Servant Leadership, and another one is respect. I would suspect that the people you worked with respected you, as well.

DENNIS: Again, I think so. This was right in the middle of the whole Bill Clinton impeachment issue, and people were tired of all that stuff. Newt couldn't get elected Speaker because, basically, he was on TV all the time and his face was out there. He would say one thing then turn around the next Sunday morning on TV and say something else. People saw that. We lost six seats in the next election, so we only had a six-vote margin, and we had eighteen people who said they weren't going to vote for Newt. So there we were with eighteen people who were not on the same page. I decided to turn back to some old coaching philosophy that I'd learned. If the coach is in the news every week, the team is in trouble. If the team is in the news every week, then they're doing pretty good. I realized that one of my fortes was serving people, getting things done, and making sure that people had the ability and opportunity to get their jobs done. I wanted to be an enabler. I tried to make sure with my speakership that I wasn't in front of the cameras all the time. Some people criticized me for that, but I tried to get the committee chairmen or people who are moving the legislation to get the recognition.

GB: So you chose not to be in the headlines?

DENNIS: Yes. I just felt that people had had enough of that. And I think they chose me because they knew I was not going to be a high profile guy but was going to work to get things done, and we did. We got an amazing amount of legislation done.

GB: Do you think Servant Leadership principles can be taught or learned or are you just born with it?

DENNIS: I look back at my circumstances, and I go back to my high school days where I had a high school coach who showed me I could do some things I never thought I could do. During my senior year of football, I was asked to help coach the linemen and was, essentially, a student coach. In college, I had another coach who took me under his wing, helped me along and gave me good guidance. When I started teaching, I had an athletic director who was very good to me and helped me a lot. I got into the legislature, and the chairman of the Revenue Committee, not much older than I was, brought me in and showed me the ropes. I came to Congress, and Bob Michel, who was the Republican leader from Ill-

173

inois at the time, was a great mentor to me. I think I learned a lot about Servant Leadership from all of those people.

So then I thought that mentoring was a very important part of my job. When I was Speaker, I'd bring in the top twenty or twenty-five young members who I could tell had a future. I would bring them in every Thursday afternoon to sit around and basically dissect what had gone on the week before. If we had problems, we would talk about how we solved them and the things we had to deal with. It was sort of a seminar every week to talk about what leadership was all about. Today a lot of those young guys like Paul Ryan are now the leaders.

GB: Would you say you demonstrate Servant Leadership principles first and then become a leader or are you a leader first who takes on Servant Leadership characteristics?

DENNIS: Everyone does things a little different. John Boehner certainly has a different style than I do. Nancy Pelosi has a different style than I did. The first thing I learned when I started coaching was that I couldn't be my old coaches. I had to be me. You earn that trust, and that trust happens over a long period of time.

GB: Obviously you can't be a coach, a teacher, or be in Congress and not face conflicts. How would you say you have used Servant Leadership characteristics or principles in the resolution of conflicts?

DENNIS: You know, I always said we had three days for legislation. Tuesdays were gridlock days—people running around with their own agendas, ideas, talking to the press when they said they wouldn't. Wednesday was where we sat them down at the table and worked out the differences, got people comfortable so they could vote for stuff. Then Thursdays, you passed legislation. It was a routine you worked with. And there were always conflicts, always some kind of crisis every week, sometimes every day. I went from meeting to meeting, started around seven-thirty in the morning and maybe would go until eight o'clock at night, and there was always something that had to be resolved. That's what the leadership was all about. I always said they called me the Speaker, but they should have called me the "Listener," because one of the ways of resolving conflict is just listening to people's problems. Sometimes, when people explain their problems, it solves itself. They find the road to solution themselves.

GB: So listening was key to your method of resolving conflicts?

DENNIS: Yes, you have to listen to people. They have to believe that you care about them and that you care about what their problems are before you can begin to resolve them. Sometimes, as you're listening, you're thinking, "Is this guy kidding? That's not a problem." Then, as they are explaining and talking it out, they realize that, too. It's a kind of catharsis for them.

GB: You just mentioned "caring," a prime characteristic of Servant Leadership. Please expound on that.

DENNIS: I always think about this guy from East St. Louis who was the forward guy for the then Speaker and he would rail and rail against farmers and union guys. This guy was just obnoxious all the time. Then one time I took the train from St. Louis up to Springfield, and the train went through this guy's district. I saw it was all old factories that were all shut down, with broken windows and people out of work. I realized then where this guy was coming from. Everyone who is elected to office comes from some place for some reason, and you have to understand why they are there, what problems they care about.

Once you start to understand the people, you start to see resolutions to the problems.

GB: Do you believe that most people who have been elected to serve have some Servant Leadership characteristics?

DENNIS: Everybody's unique. I've dealt with a lot of people who were from Harvard, Yale, and Dartmouth. They had great minds, but sometimes not a lot of common sense. Everybody has strong points, and we all have weak points. You have to understand where those strengths and weaknesses are so that you can put them in a place where they can best be used and have success. There are a lot of great people in Congress. In that position, you have to put your ego on the line every day. You put your family and your reputation on the line. You put yourself out there in front of the press. You have to lay yourself open to all of that and really feel that you have something to do, something to achieve, something to say, or a burning issue to get done. But I think you find the best people are generalists, not just one-issue people. They understand a lot of different things, and they get a lot of things done. They want to make life better for people. Then again, there are some people who are on their own ego trips, too. That's just a fact.

GB: Tell me about role models. Do you still have role models in your life, people that you look up to and want to emulate?

DENNIS: I've met a lot of good people in my life. I've read a lot, including books about Roosevelt and Lincoln and men like that. But one of the things I've always wanted to do, even when I was in the legislature, was to be in the classroom and to get kids to see that politicians are real people. Some have great attributes, some have good attributes. The key is how you handle the adversities in your life and overcome personality flaws to become a leader. It's not easy. I always felt it was important to go into the classroom and show that leaders were really just people.

GB: Dennis, last question. If you could teach young people just one thing, what would it be?

DENNIS: I talk to kids a lot, and I tell them, "You can do anything you want to, but you need to be careful. All you have to do is get in trouble once— one drug problem or arrest or something like that— and it can spoil your life. So you need to be careful. But you can do anything in life if you put your mind to it. You are only limited by yourself. Anything that is worth doing is going to be a lot of work, and there will be a price to pay for it, but you can get there."

Reflections

It was certainly interesting to interview Dennis Hastert at his getaway home in southern Wisconsin. For years, he was the third-most-important person in the country as the Speaker of the House. (The order of succession of power in this country is President, Vice President, and then the Speaker of the House.)

However, if I did not know that fact prior to going into this interview, I would never have suspected it to be the case. Dennis Hastert gave the impression of being very approachable and, certainly, not overly impressed with himself about his accomplishments and the position he once held.

It appeared to be important to him that people recognize that politicians are just people the same as we are, that they have families and friends that are important to them, just like us, and that they have their share of faults, just like us. Every person is unique. He believes it is important to look for the unique qualities in everyone.

Speaker Hastert has been a leader, in one form or another, for most of his life. Even though he didn't say this, I believe he was elevated to these positions of leadership because of his lifelong Servant Leadership personality. Because of his honesty and the trust and respect that other Congressmen had for him, he was asked to run for the position of Speaker of the House. He did not seek that position, and it seems like he was surprised by the confidence his colleagues had in him when they asked him to assume that very powerful role.

It appears that Dennis Hastert learned at a very young age that, if you are honest, loyal, and show interest in other people, all of which are Servant Leadership principles, people will follow.

It seems evident that the experience and the lessons in life he learned from the position of teaching young people in the classroom and coaching athletics served as a good training ground for becoming a Congressman.

Hearing Speaker Hastert describe his daily routine of meetings, speaking, traveling, etc., gives proof that he had a very strong work-ethic. He appeared to have the attitude that you just have to do what you have to do. As he said, it went with the territory.

Listening is described as an important ingredient of being a Servant Leader. In Speaker Hastert's words, he defines listening as being an important part of being a leader. It was amusing to hear him say that, instead of being referred to as the Speaker, it might have made more sense to be called the "Listener."

To Think About

• How would you describe your work ethic?

• Do you look for the unique qualities in everyone you meet?

• Would other people describe you as a good listener?

Servant Leadership
in ATHLETICS

What Is a Successful Leader in Athletics?

When one thinks of success in athletics, one automatically thinks of wins and losses. Those numbers are certainly an important determination of success in athletics, and, generally speaking, winning is the primary goal of anyone involved in athletics at any level of competition.

How well a coach successfully transmits the basic fundamentals of a sport to his or her athletes is a key ingredient of success. In turn, that is impacted by how much respect the players have for their coach, and the degree to which he or she builds trust, respect, and camaraderie among the team. Creating a strong desire and enthusiasm for winning is also an important ingredient that cannot be denied.

John Wooden is widely considered to be the best college basketball coach in the history of the game. He defines success this way: "Success is peace of mind, which is a direct result of self-satisfaction in knowing you did your best to become the best that you are capable of becoming."

Coaches have the unique opportunity to have

significant influence on their athletes. I believe that coaches who use Servant Leadership principles not only have a better chance of achieving success in their given sport, but have the potential to be a positive role model and to positively influence the future lives of the people they coach.

ROGER HARRING

The name Roger Harring is not an unfamiliar name in La Crosse. His name is also widely known among college football fans, sports writers, players, and coaches all across this country. The University of Wisconsin–La Crosse football field is named after him, in part because of his popularity and football successes, but also because he is respected and appreciated as a human being.

His accomplishments are numerous. He was the head football coach at UW–L for twenty-nine years. His teams won three national championships. He posted a very impressive win-loss record of 250–66–7, ranking him third in total victories and sixth in winning percentage (.785) among active NCAA Division III coaches when he retired. Harring, in his humble way, gives much of the credit for his success to a knowledgeable and experienced coaching staff. True to Harring's style, that staff guided the UW–L

Eagles to the NCAA III championship in 1992 when "Coach" was sidelined by heart surgery. Most recently, having won 261 games, Harring was named the WIAC Football All-Time Coach.

In a book written about him in 1998, *The Harring Era*, he is quoted as saying, "We recruit talented student-athletes and retain them by treating them with respect as individuals instead of just a jersey number."

Many of his former athletes speak very highly of him as a coach and mentor. They acknowledge that he meant more to them than just being the person in charge of the football program. They learned a lot about life by being on his teams.

Let's Meet Roger Harring

GB: Roger, what is your understanding of the concept of Servant Leadership?

ROGER: I'm not really sure. Basically, I just think it means I would do for others as I would have them do for me. I just think I'm a "do unto others" kind of guy. In other words, I feel strongly about helping others discover their own talents, and helping point out to an individual how to achieve that. If anybody is interested and wants to get someplace, it's important that someone recognizes that and points out their strengths to them. When you say "servant," I tend to think more in terms of a priest. I had a lot of good priests help me in my younger years in many ways. They were always there for me. I came from a broken home and, for some reason, the priests liked me and took me under their wing.

GB: I think what you're saying is that you've always tried to help others reach their potential. When you recognized that someone had some talent, do you remember thinking a lot about how you were going to help that person?

ROGER: I remember one time a young football player came into my office who was failing in his classes, and he wanted me to sign some document. He said that he needed my signature on some paper to get back into class. I signed it, and threw it on the floor, and the young man looked at me as if to say, "What was that all about?" I said, "If you don't know how to use your talents and work at getting passing grades, you are wasting my time, and you are wasting your time." With that response, the young man got up and closed the door, and he began to talk about things that were bothering him. It turned out to be a very meaningful, teachable moment.

GB: So you not only valued your football players' athletic ability, you valued them as people?

ROGER: That was my whole thing. I basically used sports as my avenue to learn how to live life, to learn right from wrong, to respect what they have, and to use it to their fullest ability. I also had many opportunities to teach and encourage young people not to be prejudiced against one another because of the color of their skin.

GB: Where do you think you learned or acquired the desire to treat people with fairness and respect?

ROGER: My grandmother had the greatest influence on my life. She was the nicest person in the world, was always a hard worker that treated everyone with equal kindness. She was just a nice person. She always said nice things to people.

GB: Successful leaders have become successful because of their ability to get other people to follow them. Was that something that you found challenging to do?

ROGER: In most ways, it felt natural. But most importantly you have to have knowledge about your craft. You have to have a strong work ethic and you have to be able to get along with people. I believe it is important to work people hard, but to make sure at the end of the day that you can put your arm around them. Another very important thing is that you have to help people to believe in themselves. If they don't believe in themselves, they will never accomplish the goals that they want to achieve.

GB: Did you ever have any unsuccessful seasons?

ROGER: I had three in high school and one in college.

GB: And how did you try to be an effective leader during a losing season?

ROGER: You have to be a stable force to your players in that kind of environment and recognize the improvements that we are making. You have to continue to be the source of encouragement and give kids the opportunity to find out what they're best at doing, to continue to give them a knowledge base that they might not be able to see in themselves.

GB: What would be your advice to a young aspiring coach?

ROGER: You have to know your craft. You have

to know what you're selling. You have to get to know people as best you can and try to find some common ground with them. Probably the most important thing is setting the example by working hard. Doing those things becomes contagious to those around you. I guess I want to be loved . . . most people do. But more important to me is that I want to be respected. My greatest reward for all of my experiences and the successes I have achieved is when my former players still contact me and just want to visit and see how I'm doing and for me to see what they are doing in their lives.

Reflections

As I reflected on my interview with Roger, it was obvious to me that it was very important for him to instill self-discipline, basic football fundamentals, and a feeling of self-confidence in his players. But how his players and assistant coaches felt about him was even more important.

Wanting other people to like and respect you seems like an obvious and very important concept of Servant Leadership. It will significantly impact how you conduct yourself. Not caring about how other people feel about you (the antithesis of caring) would eliminate any inhibition in regards to how you treat people.

It was also very interesting to note that when I asked who he thought had the most positive influence on his life, immediately and without hesitation he referred to his grandmother. His positive reflections on his grandmother were filled with strong emotions.

Roger was the first person I interviewed for this book. I thought about that interview, sensing what an incredible influence a grandmother or someone special can have on this macho athlete. Because we all have these special people in our lives, in each subsequent interview I made a conscious effort to focus on the important people in each individual's life who gave them the basis of their Servant Leadership characteristics.

Something else that I gleaned from this interview is the integrity that it takes to handle success with humility. In my opinion, responding to tremendous success with humility is a great characteristic of Servant Leadership. I believe that Roger Harring handles his success with humility, perhaps even when the temptation not to do so is strong.

To Think About

• Is it important how other people feel about you?

• Does it bother you if someone is angry or upset with you?

• Do you find yourself changing your behavior or response to a situation in order to have people like you?

BARBARA GIBSON

Entering her twenty-seventh season as gymnastics coach at the University of Wisconsin–La Crosse in 2011–12, Barbara Gibson has developed the system to continually turn out one of the most successful Division III gymnastics programs in the nation.

"As I look at the gymnastics program the last twenty-five years, UW–L's tradition and reputation of academic and athletic excellence is what has inspired me to lead the gymnastics program to national and WIAC acclaim," says Gibson. "It has been my hope to assist each of my athletes in growing and progressing personally, as well as in their sport. It has been paramount that my athletes enjoy and have fun with their passion for gymnastics. Our program has continued to progress each year, and we've been able to recruit athletes from one year to the next that can contribute to our goal, which is to finish in the top three in the country."

A former conference champion gymnast herself, who also earned academic honors, she understands the commitment and dedication the sport requires. Gibson was the 1975 Wisconsin Women's Intercollegiate Athletic Conference champion on the balance beam for UW–L. She was also the conference champion in the floor exercise in 1978.

During her twenty-six-year coaching tenure at UW–L, Gibson has led the Eagles to fifteen National Collegiate Association championships, beginning in 1986 and most recently in 2011. In addition, she has guided the Eagles to seventeen WIAC titles.

She has been named conference Coach of the Year six times, and received national honors in 1989, 2001, 2005, 2008, and 2010, when she was awarded the NCCA Coach of the Year award. She has also been recognized with the YMCA's Outstanding Achievement Award in Sports, presented to her in 1989. Her students, her athletes, and her peers have certainly acknowledged her dedication and success, and to recognize that dedication, the Barbara Gibson Endowment Fund for UW–L Gymnastics was established in her honor during the 2009–10 season.

Let's Meet Barbara Gibson

GB: Barbara, let me start by asking, What is your understanding of Servant Leadership?

BARBARA: I think it's a style of leadership that focuses more on external than internal, and what I mean is that it is more about the people that you are attempting to lead than it is about yourself. There are a number of characteristics that surround that style or approach.

GB: Would you talk a little bit more about that statement, that it is more about the people you are coaching or dealing with than yourself? Are you saying that you put the focus more on those people?

BARBARA: Absolutely. And I think it's more about those relationships and what you are attempting to build with that relationship. For me, obviously, with coaching, the relationship that I'm trying to build surrounds itself with trust. With trust comes loyalty, so there is a level of respect that is being given to them constantly. I'm dealing with eighteen to twenty-two year olds, which means these are young adults. They have good minds. They also are very driven. They are doing something they love, and there is no external reward other than what drives them internally, so I think respect is something that really goes both ways.

GB: Would you say that because your focus is on the young athletes you're coaching rather than on yourself, that those young people sense that in you? Do you think they know that you are there because it's about them?

BARBARA: Yes, I think they know that. I think you have to operate with a lot of humility and humbleness, and I think that I am a better Servant Leader now than I was as a young coach.

GB: How so?

BARBARA: Well, I don't think I had the depth of understanding of the impact that I could have. As you age and have more life experiences as a coach, you begin to see how important this human life is and the impact you can have. I always say that I can make a practice great and positive, or I can make it negative and just plain hard. I have that choice every single day, and so you are really dictating a lot of the human response based on what you're giving them. I think about some of those younger teens that I had years ago, and when I see some of them as alums, I always wrap my arms around them and groan, "Oh, you had to endure me," because I think I was out to prove something, and I'm just not like that anymore.

GB: That tells me so much already. I chose to interview you because you have created this outstanding record, and I am trying to determine how that happens. You've alluded to this already, but do you see yourself as a Servant Leader?

BARBARA: Absolutely. I learned that. I also think there are certain qualities within me that I just naturally possessed, and probably are based in the way I was raised to treat people. Part of what my parents taught me was to treat people the way I wanted to be treated. I often go back to that feeling, that human premise of kindness that I think was in me. There are other parts of being a servant leader you grow into and you learn more about. But to me, the human response, that human relationship, is key.

To give you an example, yesterday I had an expectation of an event that I was really trying to encourage: "This is what we need to get done today. This is the progress we need to have." And I had an athlete who day in and day out, ninety-eight per cent of the time, is giving me her all. She turned to me and looks at me with these big watery eyes and says, "I just can't today." And I asked what was wrong and she said, "I'm so stressed out." And I said, "What is it? Tests? School issues?" And she says, "No, I just have big-time boyfriend problems." She's never shared with me anything about her boyfriend or anything like it before. That's just something that we generally don't share a lot about. But with the relationship we shared, she knew she couldn't give it her all right then, so she had to share with me that "I just can't do this." So I hugged her and said, "Okay, today's not the day. Tomorrow will be new. No big deal. How can we make the practice productive?" So I threw the decision to her. "What do you think you can make progress on without meeting my bar? What's your bar?"

That's the relationship part I'm talking about—when you can get to that level where they trust you, but at the same time you have to keep the bar high. You can't just have the expectation that the bar is set where they can reach it all the time. You keep trying to set that goal where they still have to push.

GB: You seem to have a good understanding of what Servant Leadership is. How do you think being a Servant Leader has benefited you and those around you?

BARBARA: I think that when you give, there is a lot that you receive also. All the time. In the long-term relationships that you have—the weddings that you're going to, the notes when there are babies, the lifetime relationships—where you see the real thing that you have developed. That's the piece that you hang your hat on. Certainly, the success that we've had has been about the process that we've engaged in. We've set the bar high, we have high expectations, we're very goal-oriented, we're very hard-working and driven. All those characteristics. But in the end, it's really about the progress we're making; it's about what we're doing daily. It's not about the one day that it all comes together and happens. We've done the necessary things in the process. It's about those things we do daily, the give-and-take, how we approach our training. We can't overdo; we can't underdo. We have to figure out a pace that's right.

GB: Do you recall how old you were when you began to realize that, if you give of yourself and your values, it can come back to you in many positive ways?

BARBARA: I don't really know. I think when I realized that the way I was coaching was just so comfortable for me. I was probably ten years into it. One thing I discovered is that I had always thought everybody coached the same way. And over time, the more I interacted and even observed my own children in sports, the different things that I've seen and the behaviors that other coaches utilize, it's been really frustrating for me. I think, "Do you really think you're going to get the best out of that athlete, that young person, using those techniques?" Yes, I think I was probably in my mid-to late thirties before I really became comfortable with the way I was coaching, the way I was doing things.

GB: Have you now seen the positive results of that style?

BARBARA: Absolutely. I was hired in 1985, and we began to see success in 1995. We won Nationals in '95, then '97 and '99 and then 2001, and now we have won ten out of the last eleven. Some coaches use humiliation and negative reinforcement methods. And I can tell you, you would not find any athlete in the last ten years who would have anything to say negative about our gym. I've even had arguments with athletes who've come to UW–L from other schools and say, "I was made to do a hundreed push-ups, a hundred of this, and a hundred of that," and I always respond, "I don't use exercise as a punishment. Sorry, but that should be something you enjoy the rest of your life. So we're not going to use it in that form."

And then I'll ask them, "How bad do you want this?" Because I always think that it comes back to finding out, internally, what it is they really want and how badly they want it. I get stern. I'm not a pushover, and they know I mean business. But they also know that I'm not going to be negative and beat them up about something.

GB: Obviously, you couldn't have achieved the tremendous success you've had with the gymnastics programs at UW–L without being a successful leader. Do you feel that you are a successful leader first and then become a Servant Leader, or are your Servant Leadership skills what make you a successful leader?

BARBARA: I guess I could go either way on that question. I definitely think that being a Servant Leader is something you can learn. There are probably some basic qualities that a person has to have in order to embrace it. Maybe a more giving spirit. And perhaps that can be taught.

GB: In what ways do you think it can be taught or learned?

BARBARA: There is always the opportunity to grow. There is always the opportunity to change. So can Servant Leadership be taught? It can be taught through example. It can be taught through actions. It can be taught through expectations that you have as a leader. So it becomes a process over time. In the athletic environment, I think you are teaching a young person how to be a good teammate.

Being a good teammate is also learning how

to be a good person. It's getting outside of yourself and making the focus on someone else, seeing and recognizing that the people around you have needs. And for young people to be able to see those needs—for some of them, it's a struggle. They can go through a whole practice and not recognize any teammate's struggles. For example, there are things we do in our gym to build and foster the recognition of others' needs. There are three different groups—bars, beam, vault—and when the athletes are in that group, they have to say two things to their teammates that they did well that day. They have to share with each other. We finish practice and will sit on the floor, and I'll say, "I'd like to hear about some of the good things you saw in practice today." And in that environment, they would never say, "I did this" or "I did that." It's all about somebody else—what did someone else accomplish? So we are trying to create an environment where you are bringing them together and you have a common goal—to be our best as a team—and you ask how people are working to accomplish that.

GB: Who were some of the important people in your life and career who you feel were important in developing your values and ethics?

BARBARA: My mom and dad. My mother had a very giving spirit, and my father was very competitive. There were nine children, and they treated us all so very differently. My mother treated five daughters all very differently, based on our personalities.

My parents really shaped me. But, you know, I'm one of those people who is very reflective, probably to a fault, and I'm seeking all the time, looking for that knowledge. I always did—and do—a lot of reading. I came across a copy of *Training Camp: What the Best Do Better than Everyone Else* by Jon Gordon, and there were things in it that really rang out, so I gave all my coaches copies of that book. I always seem to be seeking out things. You can always learn something.

GB: Barbara, in your coaching career and other aspects of your life, I'm certain that you have encountered conflicts. How do you go about resolving those conflicts?

BARBARA: I'm not good at conflicts. I can tell you that right now. I don't like conflicts. I feel that I work hard at communication, because I feel that a lot of conflict results from a lack of communication. And when there's a lack of communication, there's a lack of understanding. I can see a conflict brewing on my team right now. I spoke about it at the end of practice yesterday to two assistant coaches. I told them what I had observed and that I really need to get to these two athletes, sit down and talk this thing through, because I can tell they're frustrated and they're disappointed.

GB: So what will your approach be with these two students?

BARBARA: I will get them together—maybe here after practice, or over coffee at the student union. Now with this particular conflict, I believe the first thing to do is simply open it up. "How do you feel about this?" It's going to be an open-ended question, because what I think is occurring may not be what is happening. So I really want them to talk first about what it is they are upset or disappointed about. They are seniors, and I've taken an event or two away from them, and I can tell they are not happy about it. But I need them to understand why I am doing this, and they need to tell me what impact this is having on them and where the conflict is. Their motivation is down.

When I do things, I always try to explain the "how" or the "why" behind my decision-making, and I did so to them as a group when I explained why I was taking some things away. What is happening in this situation is that they are having to sacrifice for the whole, for the good of the team. And you can see that some of them aren't buying into that right now. I can choose to ignore this problem right now, but I think the conflict will get bigger, the team chemistry will suffer and be hurt. They won't buy into the team-concept, and right now all they know is, "I don't get what I want."

My job is to represent the whole; it is not to make them all happy. And I try to tell them that you have to respect the team, respect your teammates. You don't always have to like them—but you have to respect them and the fact that they are on the same team as you are. The team is the whole, and the whole can be the best. That's my job. When I get it wrong, it's important for me to take ownership of that and to say, "I dropped the ball." It's important for those young people to see that I'm not perfect. There was a time in my career when I felt that I did have to be perfect. And quite frankly, when I let go of that, I think I became a better person and we functioned better.

GB: The last question: If you could teach one thing to young people today, what would it be?

BARBARA: Find something that you love. You can take a sport that you love and take that athletic experience to the very end, becoming a college athlete in that sport, and excelling. If you can find that same sort of love in other things, follow that. Follow that because it will bring a lot of happiness.

Reflections

There is nothing artificial about Barbara Gibson. In listening to her, it is hard to imagine that she has ever told a lie. Her genuineness is a prominent feature and one of the main Servant Leadership characteristics that I believe has helped her become a very successful gymnastics coach.

Focusing more on the people around you than on yourself is one way that she describes Servant Leadership. She also believes that humility is a key ingredient of being an effective Servant Leader. Even though she didn't say it, I know that she would subscribe to the philosophy of allowing others to sing your praises rather than yourself.

I enjoyed listening to her belief that you can teach Servant Leadership. She believes that if she treats her student athletes with Servant Leadership principles, they will learn how to incorporate Servant

Leadership principles into their own repertoire of personal behavior. She very strongly confirmed my belief on that same subject.

There is no doubt in Barbara's mind as to where she learned her philosophy of life. She is still impressed with how her parents could treat all of her eight siblings the same, but at other times differently because of their different personalities. She credits her parents with teaching her the values she tries to live by today

Her sensitivity to feelings, her genuineness of caring for people, and her ability to create in her athletes the desire to become the best they can be has resulted in a very successful career as a gymnastics coach.

Barbara gives evidence to the fact that you can be a very successful coach without being demeaning, overly critical, using harsh words, or trying to intimidate your athletes. I also suspect that her athletes have learned a lot about life in general from being under her tutelage.

To Think About

• Would you describe yourself as a genuine person?

• Do you like to be around genuine people?

• Can you think of some people that you know who are truly genuine?

Servant Leadership
in RELIGION

What Is a Successful Leader in Religion?

Coming up with my own definition of success in religion was somewhat challenging. There are not tests, measurements, wins or losses that one can use to evaluate the success of a religious leader. In my lifetime, I have been exposed to many people who occupy leadership roles in religious positions, and many, but not all of them, could be considered successful Servant Leaders.

Of course, an important criterion of a successful religious leader is how well they explain and communicate the meaning of the origin of their religious beliefs. Some successful religious leaders were born with the proverbial silver tongue, some have worked to grow in their ability to communicate effectively, and still others can make a sermon seem endless as they struggle to string words together. I have always felt that a successful religious leader was someone who could relate the Gospel through the use of analogies that are a part of current history. For me, it not only helps me better understand the teachings of the Bible, but it significantly increases my retention as I see its relevance to today's events.

In my opinion, there can never be too much importance given to how a religious leader lives his or her personal life, for in few other professions are leaders automatically assigned the job of being role models. How they "walk the talk" validates what is being said from the pulpit. If religious leaders conduct their personal lives in contrast to what they are teaching, this creates a serious scar on the religious community.

The size and growth of a particular church or church group is one way to reflect on the success of a pastor or the teaching of that denomination. A successful Servant Leader in the field of religion must motivate others to follow, to join in, and that is generally reflected in the membership numbers and even budgets of churches.

Whether you are a Christian or not, it would be hard to deny that Jesus Christ was a Servant Leader. Many people have used His words, values, and lifestyle as a basis of characteristics that they try to emulate.

PASTOR BILL HYBELS

Most people would not doubt that Servant Leadership plays an important role with religious leaders. With so many examples to choose from, I thought a lot about who would be symbolic of Servant Leadership within the realm of religion.

My wife and I have attended Willow Creek Church, in South Barrington, Illinois, on several occasions. We always left those services feeling inspired and uplifted. I also would leave wondering who started this church that now so many people call it their church home?

Bill Hybels is the founding and senior pastor of Willow Creek Community Church. The church began in 1975 with a handful of young people gathered in a rented movie theater, and today it has grown to more than 24,000 members and 18,000 people in attendance for the weekend services.

Pastor Bill has authored seventeen books, including such classics as *Too Busy Not to Pray, Becoming a Contagious Christian, Courageous Leadership,* and *The Volunteer Revolution.*

In the April 22, 2011 issue of *Parade Magazine* an article about the five largest churches in America listed Willow Creek Community Church as the fourth largest.

Let's Meet Pastor Bill Hybels

GB: Pastor Bill, thank you for taking time out of your very busy schedule to do this interview with me. I would like to begin by asking, What is your understanding of Servant Leadership?

BILL: It's kind of the mental framework that a leader has in mind when she or he approaches their leadership style, and so to me that means that, fundamentally, you feel that you are a servant to Jesus Christ, that you are a servant to the cause that he has called you to. You are a servant to the organization that you are building to achieve the cause, you are a servant to your colleagues and those who work around you, under you, and over you. Ultimately, we are going to be evaluated. Jesus said, "The last shall be first, and the first shall be last." If you want to be first in the kingdom of God, be a servant to all. So that's kind of how I view it.

GB: I've chosen you for this interview because I believe that you must use Servant Leadership in your personal and professional life, and so my question to you is, Have you or do you think of yourself as a Servant Leader?

BILL: Absolutely. I was discipled by a European

seminary college and seminary professor who, in no uncertain terms, formed leadership around servant-hood, and one of the famous passages that he would drill into my head was when Jesus said, "Do not act as others do where they lord their authority over other people. May that not be a part of how you lead." That was instilled in me before I built Willow Creek. This was a man who was one of the founding elders of our church. If he sensed any little vestige of arrogance in me, or my trying to use the church to further some-thing in my own life, it was unacceptable to him. So this was built deeply into me before I even got going in leadership. I had the advantage of this framework before I even started.

GB: How do you feel that you have applied prin-ciples and characteristics of Servant Leadership in your life, and how have they benefited those around you and yourself?

BILL: I see myself and the leadership team at Willow Creek as those who resource, energize, in-spire, and help the people on my leadership team to achieve what they've been entrusted with. In other words, when they come in to my office, I don't say, "What have you done for me lately?" I say, "How can I spend the next two-and-a-half hours furthering what it is that you've been entrusted by God and the senior leaders of our church to do?" While I wander around the church building, I ask people, "Is there any way I can use my power and influence or platform or resources to further what it is that you are doing?" So you know, it's the old upside-down pyramid thing. People in our organization don't exist to serve me. I am the chief servant at this church, existing to serve colleagues and people at all levels in the organization and ultimately, to serve everyone at Willow Creek. Now, I can't do that alone because of the scale of the church. Others have to help me. But as you know, after every service that I preach at Willow, I stand down front and I stay until every last person who I can serve in some way is served. Now, occasionally, if I have a flight I have to catch or something, I make a small exception to that, but other than that, that's my practice.

GB: And you definitely demonstrated that. It is very impressive that you take the time to do that. As I sat in the congregation that day and listened to your sermon, I thought, "Is there any way possible I could have the chance to talk to him?" You made that possible, and that's an admirable thing. Do you think a successful person becomes a leader first and then develops an attitude of serving others, or vice versa?

BILL: I've seen both. I've seen some leaders who abuse power and authority and who do everything to make the organization serve them. They never have that second conversion experience to Servant Leadership their whole career. Some of them, by earthly success standards, are wildly successful. You can't deny that. They're annoying people to be around. They have low respect levels in the organization, instill high fear levels, but they have a great product or they have a lot of external factors that make the tide go up. They spend their whole career with a high control-and-command style, and that's the way they lead. They make millions and retire to play golf. So I've seen that.

Then I've seen people who got part way through their career and said, "Who am I becoming? What am I doing? This is not the kind of leader I want to be." They have a kind of conversion experience and they say, "From this day forward, I'm going to lead another way," and they do.

Then I also see people who start right out in leadership because they've developed admirably and properly. They start out as Servant Leaders. And I've seen the opposite conversion happen. Some people start as servants, get to a certain point and flip over and say, "Okay, after twenty years of my serving this place, it is going to serve me." They trip over salaries, they get up on a little perch, lead from on high and finish out the other way. So there are a lot of models out there.

GB: Bill, have there been individuals in your life that helped shape you as a Servant Leader?

BILL: Yes, without question. My college professor who tutored and discipled me and was a founding elder at Willow Creek was that person. When he saw any telltale signs of my losing the vision of Servant Leadership, he would be unrelenting in his attempt to coach me back to center line.

GB: I am sure you have experienced situations in your life that involve personal conflict. How do you feel you have been able to apply Servant Leadership principles in resolving those conflicts?

BILL: You know, whenever a leader leads something with moving parts or moving people, which all organizations experience, there's going to be friction. So every leader deals with the inevitable friction that is caused by organizational movement. What I have been tutored in and what I have tried to train myself to do—and this phrase is very, very important to me—when someone in the organization disappoints me, when I learn of stress cracks or whatever, I try to move toward the conflict rather than away from it. I try to move quickly, as opposed to letting stuff build up over time. And my opening comment—and this is the phrase that I've tried to imbed into our entire culture—my opening comment usually is, "Please help me understand." "Please help me understand why you blew through your budget. Please help me understand why that assignment got dropped. Please help me understand why you were late four times last week. Please help me understand why you lost your temper in that meeting."

So instead of my starting with an accusation where there's conflict, I start with a question, assuming that this wonderful person has a rational and justifiable explanation. So to this person, I say, "Please help me understand why you were late four times last week," and he or she may respond by saying, "Well, I had to put my son in a treatment program," or "My wife was sick, and I had to take the kids to preschool." It offers an opportunity for someone to give a comfortable answer and to immediately reduce the conflict. I've tried to train our whole organization to use that phrase. "Please help me to understand, and I'm sure you can," and we'll move from there. Now, still sometimes conversations get very tough if there are not good answers, and sometimes there has to be a redefinition of what our values are.

GB: Bill, I want to thank you for taking time out of your busy schedule to conduct this interview with me.

BILL: It has been my pleasure, and good luck to you.

Reflections

I have discovered that my interviews with Servant Leaders are a very enjoyable exercise in gaining a better understanding of the attitudes and concepts that each person uses to demonstrate and facilitate the concept of a Servant Leader. It seems that in each interview there is at least one particularly good idea or concept that emerges.

How Bill answered the question, "How do you use Servant Leadership principles in resolving conflicts?" intrigued me. He said that he liked to solve conflicts as soon as possible, and when he faces them, his first question is, "Could you please help me understand how it is that you have been late several days this week, why you raised your voice in our meeting, why you are angry with so-and-so, etc." I think this is an excellent Servant Leadership principle to employ when looking to solve problems. It defuses the anger in the person to whom you are talking. It is a nonthreatening way for you to approach a sensitive subject. It obviously demonstrates that you are concerned, that you care, and it is a compassionate way of beginning the process of resolving the problem. What it does not do is stoke the sparks of defensiveness. The question does not encourage the individual to defend him or herself. Defensiveness does not positively contribute to solving problems, so any way to remove it from the equation is beneficial.

Of course, Bill said many other important things, as well. It was interesting when I asked him if he thought he was a Servant Leader, he confidently and without hesitation said, "yes." I am quite sure that most Servant Leaders, if asked and given time to think about it, would also answer "yes" as confidently. However, Bill knows, and has a good understanding of how his Servant Leadership principles have contributed to his success and that of Willow Creek Community Church.

To understand what it means to be and act like a Servant Leader can often serve as an impetus and motivation to use those principles more often. Like exercise, using principles of Servant Leadership can help you grow, only instead of strengthening muscles, you are strengthening your ethics and compassionate nature.

I encourage you to not be embarrassed or shy about recognizing the Servant Leadership principles that you practice in your life. Just keep doing it!

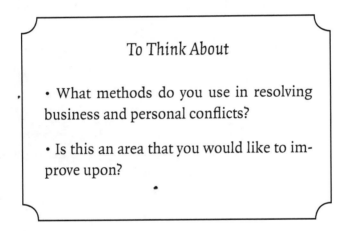

To Think About

• What methods do you use in resolving business and personal conflicts?

• Is this an area that you would like to improve upon?

A Little Side Trip

In October of 2011, Betty and I participated in a pilgrimage to Assisi, Italy. For nine days, we studied and learned about the life of St. Francis. It was an incredible experience to learn about the philosophy and teachings of this religious leader. After thoroughly looking into the life of this fascinating person for nine days, I felt like I had a good understanding of the way Francis of Assisi thought and taught. Therefore, I decided to do a make-believe interview with St. Francis, attempting to answer my own questions the way I thought St. Francis would answer them. Please keep in mind that the following interview is based on my interpretation, and I have, indeed, taken poetic license. While we do not have writings from the man that are specific to the concept of Servant Leadership, it is my opinion that St. Francis was a true and pure Servant Leader.

SAINT FRANCIS OF ASSISI

Francis di Bernardone was born in 1182 in Assisi, Italy. He was an Italian Catholic Friar and preacher, founding the men's Franciscan Order, the women's

Order of St. Clare, and the lay Third Order of Saint Francis. St. Francis is one of the most venerated religious figures in history.

Francis was the son of a wealthy cloth merchant in Assisi. He lived the high-spirited life typical of wealthy young men of that period and later fought as a soldier for Assisi. While going off to war in 1204, Francis had a vision that directed him back to Assisi, and he found that he had lost his taste for his worldly life. On a pilgrimage to Rome, he lived with the beggars at St. Peter's, and that experience moved him to live in poverty. Francis returned home, began preaching on the streets, and soon amassed a large following.

His order was endorsed by Pope Innocent III in 1210. He then founded the Order of Poor Clares, which was an enclosed order for women, as well as the Third Order and Sisters of Penance. By this point, the Franciscan Order had grown to such an extent that its primitive organizational structure was no longer sufficient. He returned to Italy to organize the order. Once his organization was endorsed by the Pope, he began to withdraw from external affairs.

Anyone who has ever set up a manger scene at Christmas has been touched by St. Francis, as he arranged for the first display in 1223. In 1224, he received the stigmata, making him the first person to bear the wounds of Christ's passions, and two years later, while preaching Psalm 141, he died on October 3, 1226. Less than two years later, he was pronounced a saint by Pope Gregory IX.

St. Francis is known as the patron saint of animals and the environment and one of the two patrons of Italy (with Catherine of Siena). It is customary for both Catholic and Anglican churches to hold ceremonies blessing animals on his feast day of October 4.

An (Imagined) Interview with Francis of Assisi

GB: Francis [he was not declared a Saint until after his death] would you please explain to me your understanding of the concept of Servant Leadership?

FRANCIS: I am sorry to disappoint you, but I don't know what you mean by putting these two words, "Servant" and "Leadership," together.

GB: I will try to explain this new and upcoming relational concept. Servant Leadership is comprised of many characteristics that are desirable in relating to others. For example, a desire to serve others is a strong component of Servant Leadership. Being trustworthy, respectful, and honest with everyone are also anchors of the concept. Additionally, his desire to help others become the best they can be also defines and characterizes the concept of Servant Leadership.

FRANCIS: Ah! I think I see now what you mean by Servant Leadership. I certainly have strong feelings and desires about being a servant. It is my belief that my purpose here on earth is to serve others, and, because of that drive and the fact that I have dedicated my life to that purpose, I guess I could be thought of as a servant.

I do have some difficulty with the terms "leader" and "leadership." I did not set out in life to become a leader or to be cast into a leadership role. It is still amazing to me that I have such a large group of followers (people who profess to have the same emotions, beliefs, and attitudes toward life that I do). I have discovered, however, that once people subscribe to and follow your beliefs, they do have a need to be given direction and guidance. I guess that since so many people are now looking for and seeking my guidance that you could say I am looked upon as a leader and required to give leadership.

Now that I have tried to answer your questions

as best I can, I can see how those two words "Servant" and "Leadership" have a natural connection to each other.

GB: I have chosen you for this interview because you impress me as someone who practices Servant Leadership in your daily life. Now that you better understand the concept, do you think you are a Servant Leader?

FRANCIS: Without trying to bring attention to myself, I guess I could say that I am a Servant Leader. My whole purpose in life is to bring attention to God and to the teachings and leadership of His Son, Jesus Christ. Because I am so dedicated to understanding His purpose in life and trying to convey that purpose to others, I guess I could humbly say that I am a Servant Leader. But in saying so, I would like to add that I believe a person becomes a Servant Leader because of the way in which they lead their life. Being called a Servant Leader does not come simply because of your desire to become a Servant Leader; rather, it comes because others witness you making your beliefs real. The way you live resonates with them and creates in them a desire to become like you, sharing your respect for people, your compassion.

GB: What person or persons in your life have most helped shape you as a Servant Leader?

FRANCIS: I am happy to respond to that question. Of course, I learned a lot from my mother and father in my early years. I frequently watched and observed the way my father so positively dealt with his customers. Those who bought from him liked him because of the way they were treated. However, through contemplation and prayer, it is Jesus Christ who has become my role model and mentor. I have such a love for Him that I am desperately trying to pattern my life after Him. Of course, even as I try to pattern my life after Jesus Christ, I know it is impossible to become like Him. But you asked me who was my mentor, and, without any doubt, that would be Jesus Christ. I guess I could also say that my good friend Clare is a present mentor of mine. It is so enlightening to me to watch the way she tends to the sick. She is so caring and willing to give of herself to those who are less fortunate than herself.

To further answer your question, I think it is important that we all have role models and mentors in life. I believe it is important to find people who live their lives according to the way we would like to live our own and use them as an example.

GB: I am sure you have had some conflicts in your life. Do you think you have used Servant Leadership principles in trying to resolve conflicts?

FRANCIS: That is a difficult question for me to answer. First of all, I try all means of avoiding conflicts. I hate conflict. Earlier in my life, I would try to avoid conflict by hiding from it. Literally hiding. Once, in an attempt to avoid conflict with my father, I hid for one month.

I think I have matured in that area. Being cast into a role of leader, it is impossible to avoid all conflict. I now find that it is not beneficial for anyone to deny the reality of conflict. However, if conflict is dealt with by being respectful and compassionate to those with whom we disagree, most anger tends to dissipate. Of course, exercising the art of listening is a given and a must, and then ultimately we have to be forgiving. I am not sure we can ever totally forget the disagreements we have, but we can certainly put them into the back of our minds.

GB: Do you think that a person becomes a leader first and then develops an attitude of serving others or vice versa?

FRANCIS: Having answered your first question

makes it somewhat easier to answer this question. I have found that it is possible to be a leader without living by the characteristics of Servant Leadership and abiding by those principles. During the earlier days of my life, many people followed my immature and careless lifestyle. So I guess I believe that you can become a leader without being a servant. On the other hand, I also believe that if you are truly a servant and you conduct your life by purposely living your life to respond to the needs of other people, without a hidden agenda, that they will observe it and that, in turn, will create a desire for them to follow your lead.

My answer was confusing, wasn't it? I will try to be more lucid. I believe if you sincerely want to serve, the characteristics of a leader will rise in a simultaneous manner. I also believe that the vertical assent of someone who possesses leadership qualities, without the desire to serve, can be matched by the speed of their descent.

GB: If you could teach young people one thing, and one thing only, what would it be?

FRANCIS: I think that I would suggest to young people to study the words and teachings of Jesus Christ and attempt to be true to Him. My life has certainly given testament to the fact that it takes some time to discover what that means. During our youth, it is difficult, perhaps even impossible, to know and understand what our purpose in life is.

So I would suggest to young people to use patience and time to find their answers to the meaning of life for them, but I would also suggest that Jesus Christ has given us a very good road map to follow. I would also caution and forewarn young people that everyone, including family members, may not always understand what motivates you.

Additionally, I would tell them that if you are doing good deeds in the world by showing respect, being honest, encouraging others, listening and responding to the needs of others, that you will be positively rewarded.

Even though I intentionally chose a life of poverty, I do not believe it is necessarily wrong for people to acquire wealth. It is how we live our lives, whether we use the gifts of poverty or the gifts of financial abundance to serve others, that determine how we will be judged. My belief is firm that my God and my Savior are my ultimate judges.

Reflections

Having studied St. Francis during our pilgrimage in Italy, it was not that difficult for me to attempt to answer my own questions the way I thought he would answer them. I tried desperately not to impose my own values onto him.

St. Francis was quite different from all of the other people I interviewed. Because he lived a life of contemplation and much of it was in solitude, he probably had a better understanding of his purpose and meaning in life than most of us do. His devotion and focus on his purpose in life have few equals.

As was true during the time of his life, I would suspect that it would also be true today that many people would have a difficult time understanding him. I don't think he was your typical neighbor, but most likely would still be called a Servant Leader today.

I admire his conviction. I think it was his unwavering dedication to being true to Jesus Christ by serving the needy and the poor that caused so many people to gravitate to him.

The fact that so many of his teachings are remembered, and that so many buildings and institutions are named after him, give evidence to the positive way he physically and emotionally touched people during his time on earth.

It is that kind of dedication to your beliefs and values that creates a long-standing legacy and earns you the right to be called a Servant Leader.

To Think About

• What kinds of convictions do you believe in wholeheartedly?

• Do you ever spend any time in contemplation?

The Journey Is Coming
to an End

"You have arrived at your destination," says the easy-to-understand voice of my mental GPS.

Wow, what a journey this has been! This will be among the best emotional experiences in my life. I not only enjoyed the result of learning so much about the relatively new concept of Servant Leadership, but, more importantly, I enjoyed the process. Interviewing the people I have included in this journey was an incredibly rewarding experience. It was gratifying to listen to their reflective and revealing answers. And I think the people I interviewed found it to be equally enjoyable . . . at least it appeared that way.

One of my many discoveries was that successful Servant Leaders like to share their experiences about how they got where they are today. It was enjoyable to see and hear the satisfaction in their voices as they described how Servant Leadership principles played a key role in their rise to the positions they hold in life today.

Some of them had a vague understanding of the concept of Servant Leadership prior to my meeting with them, and I think the interview allowed them to

233

form a clearer picture of what characteristics constitute a servant leader. Several seemed happy to have a name or a description assigned to beliefs that they had always held and practiced, almost a validation of their chosen path.

I purposely asked each of my interviewees the same questions. In doing so, it helped me to listen for specific similarities and differences. As a result of that strategy, I am convinced that there are many more similarities than differences in the personalities of Servant Leaders. Honesty, respectfulness, loyalty, trustworthiness, hard work ethic, and encouragement of others were very similar in everyone. The main difference seemed to be the way in which these characteristics are displayed. There appeared to be some differences in the area of humility and self-confidence. However, the fact that there are differences in no way detracts from the basic tenants of Servant Leadership. It simply shows that those traits can manifest themselves in many different ways.

To the wide array and variety of personalities of the people reading this book it should be comforting to know that the manner in which Servant Leadership characteristics are practiced is not as important as possessing them. While subscribing to the characteristics of Servant Leadership principles will not necessarily guarantee success, it will certainly move you in that direction.

Before and during the writing of this book, I asked over one-hundred people outside of the La Crosse area what their understanding of Servant Leadership was. Not one person recognized the term or had anything more than a vague idea of what it meant. Not one. In most cases, my question triggered a blank look. While this surprised me somewhat, it reinforced my belief that we need to champion the cause, and promote a better understanding of this potentially life-changing concept.

As I traveled on this journey, I often thought about some people who have become successful leaders, but who have not practiced Servant Leadership principles. One of my interviewees described such people as standing on quicksand. This is so true. I have observed some leaders whose lack of ethics, understanding, a moral compass, has left them sinking into the ground. In fact, it brought to mind someone I know who was over-endowed with charisma, became very successful at a very young age, and then spent several years of his life behind bars because of making so many wrong choices in his life. Perhaps if this person had combined Servant Leadership principles with his charisma, there would have been no limit to the success he could have achieved.

During this journey, I feel like I learned things about myself, as well. It made me think about some of my weaknesses and, conversely, it confirmed some of my strengths. As we began this journey together, it was my goal that we would all have a better idea of what Servant Leadership is all about and what it means to be a Servant Leader. I have made my best attempt at trying to answer this question for myself, as hopefully you will try to answer it for yourself.

If you practice Servant Leadership principles long enough, and you sustain those characteristics enthusiastically, you have the greatest opportunity to not only be happy in doing what you do, but you will also achieve success. Being a Servant Leader does not always mean that you gain great financial worth. But you will know that you have been a good servant by the way people respond to you, and in the long run, that is what really matters in life. Servant Leadership should be the concept and provide the road map for the basis of how we conduct our lives. It should hold high prominence in who we strive to be, and it should be the example to which we hold ourselves accountable.

In some ways, I like to think that this journey falls into the category of a self-help book. I did not begin this journey with that intention. However, as I participated in and listened to what all of my very enthusiastic interviewees had to say, it has changed my mind. All of them offered such good insight and professed to so many values and ethics that positively contributed to their lives. In essence, they have given all of us an affirmation of the virtues that we should strive to incorporate into our own lives.

I hope you learned something that has motivated you to make Servant Leadership a part of your life, whether in your personal, social, or business relationships. If there was just one positive thing that you gleaned from being on this journey with me, then I have accomplished my ultimate goal. It certainly has had a positive, catalytic effect on me, and just knowing that we have shared a period of personal discovery together is a source of gratification.

Even though the concept of Servant Leadership is relatively new, to be a Servant Leader is something everyone should strive for, a character definition that everyone can, and should, utilize in the measurement of their own lives.

I think it would be difficult for anyone to be critical of the attributes of Servant Leadership. If we all would spend more time focusing on the servant leaders of the world, those people who make the needs and concerns of others their primary focus, the world would be much better for it.

Individually, we cannot positively change the world; but, collectively, if we all aspire to use and promote the concept of Servant Leadership, we can make a positive impact.

Give someone a warm fuzzy today, and when someone gives you a warm fuzzy, please pass it forward.

Afterword

This Is a Test

Shortly after making the decision to write this book, a very interesting experience presented itself to me. Betty and I were vacationing in Puerto Vallarta, Mexico. We have been going there for twenty years during the month of March. Several years ago we decided to drive an inexpensive car down to the location of our condo. We had a place on the grounds of the complex that we invested in seventeen years ago where we could store the car when we were not there. The car was a 1996 Dodge Stratus. With a few minor repairs, it had served us well for five years. However, during the spring of 2011 while we were there, Betty and I made the decision to sell this car and move on to something else. We did not advertise our car "for sale," nor did we put a "for sale" sign on the car itself.

As we were parking it one day, (after having made the decision to sell it), a young native Mexican man approached us and said his father was interested in buying a car like ours. He inquired if we might consider selling it. Rather astonished by this "happenstance" situation, Betty and I shared a smiling glance, and I told him, "Yes, we would." He then asked me how much we wanted. Not having given this much thought yet, I quickly ran some figures through my mind and responded to him that we would sell it for $1200. With his father standing in the background, he said he would get back to me in a couple of days.

This took place on a Sunday. Four days went by without our hearing from him or seeing him again. During those four days, a very nice young local resident whom I had gotten to know over the past several years, (he gave tennis lessons and arranged for court times), informed me that his car had just been stolen. This caused him and his family some undue hardship. He told me that it now took his daughter forty-five minutes to get to school via three bus exchanges instead of ten minutes when he took her to school by car. I informed Betty about my conversation with Alex, and together we decided that we would give our car to this financially disadvantaged young father.

The next day, I informed Alex about our decision, which prompted a surprised look and a very happy response. I asked him if he wanted to drive our car around the grounds before he decided if he wanted to accept our offer. After he checked out the car for about ten minutes, we once again parked it where it had been. As we were getting out of the car, the young man who had asked about buying the car the previous Sunday was waiting for us. He had the equivalent of $1200 in pesos in his hand. His father had decided to purchase our car. What should I do? What would you do?

The moment caught me by such surprise that I couldn't help but think that a "Servant Leadership" moment had just presented itself to me. I was amazed by the coincidence of the moment. There was really no question in my mind as to how I was going to handle this situation. I informed the young man with the cash in his hand that the car was no longer for sale. Once again, a big smile appeared on Alex's face. There was no question about what I should do, simply because it was the right thing to do.

A good and yet simple definition of Servant Leadership is doing what you think is the right thing to do and feeling good about the decision you make. In most situations, in our dealing with other people, it is usually pretty obvious about what is the right thing to do. And, in most cases, doing the right thing creates a positive and warm feeling.

After this experience, the thought ran through my mind that this was a test, a test to see whether or not I "walk the talk." I am sure you have also been tested from time to time when you are given more than one choice of responses to a situation. In my case, it was a choice of receiving monetary gain or helping out a disadvantaged person.

The next day after our transaction took place, Alex asked if he could get together with Betty and me. He presented us with two very thoughtful gifts. I will never forget the warm and appreciative look on his face. The memory of his look and his appreciative words far out-weighed $1200 in cash. "Doing the right thing" is the right thing to do. "Doing the right thing" is Servant Leadership in action.

Made in the USA
Lexington, KY
13 July 2013